Ana,

I hope you enjoy
the stories.

Bob

How to Climb a 12-Foot Wall

10 Military Lessons in Leadership

How to Climb a 12-Foot Wall

10 Military Lessons in Leadership

Colonel G R Pearce MBE

Illustrations by Piscator

HALSGROVE

First published in Great Britain in 2021

Copyright © Colonel G R Pearce MBE

British Library Cataloguing-in-Publication Data
A CIP record for this title is available from the British Library

ISBN 978 1 90655 149 0

Halsgrove
Halsgrove House,
Ryelands Business Park,
Bagley Road, Wellington, Somerset TA21 9PZ
Tel: 01823 653777   Fax: 01823 216796
email: sales@halsgrove.com

Part of the Halsgrove group of companies
Information on all Halsgrove titles is available at: www.halsgrove.com

Printed and bound in India by Parksons Graphics Ltd

Contents

Foreword

Foreword by Phillip Stapleton,
Headmaster West Buckland School.

I thought this was an excellent read: 10 powerful messages told with honesty and humour. The stories are immediately engaging and even more effective if you have experience of the military or leadership.

The messages are neatly summarised, well ordered (as you might expect), and provide an insight to Bob's habits as well as providing nuggets for leaders in all spheres and at all levels.

After eleven years of leadership I found of myself nodding to each anecdote and scribbling down at least one lesson from each chapter; for example, I loved question 4.

We are likely to have differing views of the style of leadership nurtured in the military but Bob stops us from falling into the trap of thinking there is no possible crossover into civvy street. There is plenty and in this book Bob provides a wonderful distillate of lessons learnt that are as relevant as they are impressive.

A brilliant handbook for the curious and aspiring leader.

The writing of this book was encouraged
by my friend Andrew St George, author of
The Navy Way of Leadership
with
illustrations by *Piscator*

The Power of Stories

I should start this book with the phrase, 'once upon a time' for that, I remember from my childhood days, is how all good tales begin.

In his book, *The Story Telling Animal* Jonathan Gottschall tells us that stories infiltrate everything we do. Stories are the fabric of our social lives, how we communicate, how we organise, how we think, how we interact. Stories help us understand, remember, engage with others and alter our own behaviour.

How many of us immediately recall an incident in our own lives when listening to somebody recount a tale about theirs? It is a natural thing to do and indeed an internal struggle not to interrupt with 'a similar thing happened to me' comment? The illustration of experience through a short story is a fundamental element of our learning. Fairy tales, parables, fables and folk stories are used to help shape behaviour, teach youngsters to recognise right from wrong and simply help us all make sense of the world.

I remember reading *How to Win Friends and Influence People* by Dale Carnegie, it was full of illustrative stories to embellish the lessons he wanted his readers to take away. The leadership books I most value have been those with short illustrations that helped me recall or remember the issue being discussed. John Kotter, known for his books on leadership and change recognised the value of stories, 'Over the years I have become convinced that we learn best and change, from hearing stories that strike a chord within us.'

During a Harvard Lecture on the NHS Executive Fast Track Programme I rediscovered the power of storytelling. Healthcare systems across the world use patients' stories as a means of conveying messages with a reality and impact hard to ignore. Having heard personal stories from a number of patients, relatives, and carers I wondered whether the same approach would help to illustrate experiences of leadership. I found that I was drawn to my Army experiences when trying to address a challenge myself or to discuss an approach with a colleague. While sometimes such storytelling might be dismissed as yet another 'war story' it seemed a valuable tool for conveying ideas, and through the use of metaphor, giving examples and changing how people thought.

Stories can really change people.

In 2014, after thirty-six years in the Army I resigned my commission to join the NHS. Just before I left I had an interview with Lieutenant General Tim Evans. I had known him from previous tours and it was a real privilege to have him give his time to a discussion about my future. I recall a particular point he made when we talked about my Master's Degree work on leadership and my move to the NHS. He talked about transferable skills and his view that how we lead in the Army may well be quite different to how people respond to leadership in the NHS, or indeed in other walks of life.

The shock of capture was significant and the difference in the way the two organisations operate was quite marked. I soon recognised however, that while there were clear differences there were indeed many personal experiences that were transferable to the NHS and possibly to other sectors too.

After three and a half years, I changed direction and now work in a school. Storytelling continues to be a valuable method of learning and I find myself calling upon the lessons of my Army experience and applying them to a variety of situations every day, including the occasional assembly!

Going 'over the top' as a military term, may not mean the same to other organisations. In the NHS we focused on the patients we wanted to help rather than an enemy we wished to defeat. The daily delivery of a high standard of service, when faced with serious challenges, insufficient information and a feeling that resources are stretched to the limit, requires strong leadership to deliver quality outputs in all sectors. I suspect the situation is similar in many commercial organisations too and the foundations of leadership are not that different when we look at what we are all trying to achieve; essentially getting people to do their very best on a bad day when nobody is looking. In the following series of short stories I highlight some of the key leadership lessons I have learned over a long career. These are not stories of great daring but observations and reflections of someone who has had the privilege to work with extraordinary people. They are short illustrations from a long career that might help leaders in any sector reflect on the situation they are facing or the decision they are about to make.

Whatever sector you may be operating in, at work or at leisure, starting out in a leadership position or setting up a coaching or training activity, I hope this collection of personal stories may help to shape your approach. They reveal why people do things and how we can inspire them to do more or better for our organisations and our bottom line (a patient, a customer, a client, a pupil or indeed a profit margin).

Where these lessons come from

My school report from the very first reception class at the age of six, states that:

> 'Robert prefers a group activity to an individual occupation. Special interests are clay-modelling, painting and the sand-pit.'

Clearly a focus on team-work and a deployment to Iraq were already on the cards.

My Army career started when I joined as a sixteen-year-old apprentice chef, travelling to the 'Home of the British Army' in Aldershot by train; I was greeted by a stereotypical Army Sergeant shouting for a group of us to hurry up; we then waited for another train before setting off for the barracks. After two years at the Army Apprentices College I became a qualified (B2) chef and was promoted to the rank of Apprentice Regimental Sergeant Major, proudly commanding 400 Junior Soldiers on the Pass Out Parade.

Just before the end of my apprenticeship I went through a rigorous interview process at the Regular Commissions Board. Supported by the Apprentices College, I attended a very challenging three-day selection event. Success meant that my posting to Germany as a private soldier was cancelled and I set off to attend the Royal Military Academy at Sandhurst as an officer cadet.

Commissioned at the age of nineteen, I found myself back at the Apprentices' College as a Platoon Commander, a strange feeling, having passed out as a private soldier only a year before.

The next big step in my career was passing the promotion to Major exams; these included selection for Staff College. Staff College was a significant step for any young officer and a particular opportunity for me as the Army formed the Royal Logistic Corps[1] during my time there which opened up far more appointments to me after completing the course. Following a series of staff appointments I commanded a Supply Squadron with the Allied Command Europe Mobile Force (Land) (AMF(L)), a unit on constant stand-by to deploy in support of NATO. Later I commanded a Transport Regiment, which included deployment to the Iraq War in 2003. Promotion to full Colonel followed with my first appointment as Commander Logistic Support in the deployable 3 (UK) Division and then Chief of Staff in HQ 5 Division before my final appointment as Chief of Staff in the Enabling Command, part of the NATO Allied Rapid Reaction Corps.

A chance reading of a national newspaper advertising the NHS Executive Fast track Programme led me to resign my commission and embark on a period as a manager in the Health Service. After another change of direction I now work as the Bursar in a school.

The NHS Fast Track Programme started with a residential element at Harvard University in Boston for a month followed by a nine month

---

1   Formed in 1993 from the Royal Corps of Transport, Royal Army Ordnance Corps, Royal Pioneer Corps, Army Catering Corps and Royal Engineers Postal and Courier Regiment.

placement in an Acute Trust where I was responsible for writing the plan to transform the Trust into a Seven Day Services compliant organisation.

Throughout my Army career I have been interested in leadership, from the very start when I was promoted to Apprentice rank, through the Royal Military Academy at Sandhurst where the fundamentals of leadership are taught to every Army officer and subsequently in a range of command appointments. I have written articles on leadership for Army and Royal Logistic Corps publications, been the senior mentor for the NATO senior logistics course and studied leadership for my MSc in 2013. While working in the NHS I continued my links with the NHS Leadership Academy, presenting to a cohort of attendees on the various leadership courses, recording short talks and by writing a weekly blog about my first year in the NHS.

Stepping onto that Aldershot train seems a long time ago; but looking back through my career I have noticed particular times when by design or indeed just good fortune I have managed to get out of scrapes, improve situations, introduce major changes or simply engender a sense of pride and energy to do things better. All by using what I had learned about leadership. So, this series of personal stories illuminate the lessons I have learned over nearly forty years; my hope is that they will prompt thinking and help those facing similar challenges in other walks of life.

Learning Lessons

An interesting observation about the difference between an organisation that deploys on a battlefield or theatre of war to do its work and one that is continually delivering a high tempo output is the matter of down-time. In the Army, we spend a great deal of our time preparing for operations and analysing and learning from them afterwards. The period of time deployed on operations is relatively short, concentrated and focused. While it is what we are all about, it does not constitute the majority of our work. In contrast, in the Health Service we are 'on operations' all the time and as a consequence there is less opportunity to learn lessons. Indeed, in my final job in the Army I was working in a NATO Corps Headquarters which had a whole branch dedicated to 'Lessons Learned'. There was a robust process whereby on a monthly basis the Chief of Staff, a Major General, spent some hours going through the key lessons we learned from exercises and operations. The aim was to make sure there was both intelligent review and strong momentum in the process of getting the best from our recent experiences. The Health Service and no doubt many other organisations 'run-hot' and have little time to reflect and learn but I think it is important to make that time; to make progress we must learn properly from our lessons.

Learning lessons contributes to personal development. Reflecting on my leadership 'journey', I believe there is value in seeing your leadership style as something you invest in and build; the foundations are the courses, programmes and research you do throughout your career. Added to that is the experience you gain from putting these skills into practice and from seeing and working with others. Your leadership style will evolve; it will slowly develop as you gain experience, to meet the needs of the environment you are operating in at the time.

Experience takes time

Having served as an apprentice for two years, I had some advantages when I turned up at Sandhurst. Tradition had it that the night before their final parade, the senior intake would tear around the place creating havoc. Early in my time, I was lying in my bed when I heard a commotion. I could hear that a group of 'seniors' was making its way down the corridor letting off CS gas (tear gas) and people were running from their rooms. I reached for my respirator and lay down on my bed; as they passed I opened my window and waited for the smoke to clear, then went back to sleep.

But not all my previous experience was helpful. Having learned to press my uniform and shine (or bull) my boots and shoes as an apprentice I was in a privileged position when it came to our guard duty system. We had to parade for inspection at the start of the weekend guard duty and always paraded with one extra person. On inspection the smartest officer cadet would be stood-down from the guard duty and more often than not, I was selected.

This advantage back-fired somewhat one day when we were on a formal parade inspection being conducted by the Academy Sergeant Major, the most senior soldier in the British Army. Coming from a Guards' Battalion he was known for his particularly smart turnout and he moved through the ranks making derogatory comments about the presentation of each officer cadet. He stood in front of me and paused. He then complimented me for my smart uniform and said he was particularly impressed with the shine on my boots. He then asked which Regiment I was going to join and in my naïve way, I told him honestly, that I was to join the Army Catering Corps. He thought I was being sarcastic, the smartest Regiments in the Army are known to be the Guards Regiments and here was this officer cadet suggesting he was to join the ACC. He then barked, 'lock him up, lock him up' and I was marched off the parade square in double-time, straight into the guard room!

The moral of the story is not to be dishonest at all, but sometimes to understand the context of the situation; in hindsight, my response might well have been something along the lines that I had yet to make my final decision.

Leadership is not a binary or two-dimensional application of the recommendations or experience of others; if only it was that simple. I have seen many people return from a leadership course; they alter their behaviour to deliver what they perceive is the intended outcome but miss the finer quality of the learning; application is much more than just repetition. There is a fundamental element to the whole business of leadership which is probably best summed up in the German word 'fingerspitzengefühl' which roughly translates to mean an 'intuitive instinct about any given situation and to know how to react to it without having to deliberate'; it also suggests a certain tact or sensitivity that comes with experience and was often used by my Instructor at the

Army Staff College[2] when describing the actions and exploits of the senior military leaders we were studying.

Leadership is not the mechanical application of lessons, either. The true craft of leadership is the ability to blend those tools and lessons with skill, judgement, intelligence, intuition, timing and a general 'feel' for how to use them in your particular environment.

Having now worked in a school for a period my thinking about these lessons has continued to develop. In the same way one would view the difference between applied and pure mathematics I think there is a parallel with the theory of leadership lessons and the practical application of them. Reading and learning the lessons in this book is only the start, applying, testing and reviewing is the real, more significant and productive element of the overall approach. If at first you don't succeed, try, try again!

There are some key leadership themes that reflect the way I have developed and got things done in the Army which translate very easily into the Health Service and indeed may prove equally successful in other arenas. Some people make assumptions about Army leadership, supposing that it is no more than the barking of orders and the strict 'command and control' approach; but they are surprised when I say that is rarely the way we do business in the military. The softer skill of understanding people and motivating them is at the heart of military leadership. Here I offer some lessons and some experience, but the real value is in your intelligent application, the blending of these and other personal experiences to shape your own leadership style.

How to use this book

When I shared a draft of this book I found that people did two things; firstly they made very helpful observations about the layout and approach and secondly, nearly all highlighted, underlined or put a big tick next to aspects that particularly resonated with them. It was because of this I thought it may be useful to write a short piece about

---

2   Lieutenant Colonel and, later Major General (Retired) Mungo Melvin CB OBE and Senior Visiting Research Fellow at King's College London.

my intent when writing the book in this way. The concept was to be able to share both my very positive and indeed negative learning experiences in a light and easy to read format in order to enable people to avoid some of the pitfalls and challenges of leadership, as well as provoking thought and evaluation. You have now read the first chapter which provides the background and an explanation of where these personal lessons come from.

The lessons have been structured under ten headings in order to provide a logical flow. I believe that these are lessons of 'applied leadership' rather than simply offering a theory and hope the stories help form a picture for others to apply in their daily approach. Each chapter starts with an explanation or notion and then summarises the lessons in a series of principles. These principles can be applied to other walks of life and may help to engender the 'esprit de corps' I have enjoyed in the Army.

Lesson	Summary
1	Start with the end in view
2	Leadership is a full time job
3	You can't climb a 12-Foot wall on your own
4	We all need a sentry to guard us when we sleep
5	Stand still right or wrong
6	Hold your nerve
7	The cost of leadership is self-interest
8	Treat others as you wish to be treated
9	Time spent in reconnaissance is seldom wasted
10	Sometimes we all need the patience of a sniper

I have put the lessons in a form of order and recommend that getting an overview of the whole book is the best initial approach. Reading in detail and then reflecting or reaching for it when something is happening to you at the time, or making a note about something you can draw upon later. The best way to do this is to mark the page as you read, highlight the passage, draw lines under key thinking or comments and add flags or bookmarks to make it easier to find things. I have not got a solution to every issue and you may indeed cross things out that do not apply, but I aim for the stories to help focus the mind. Having a marked or annotated copy may be useful when you come across a situation or need to prepare for something and recall reading about it here. There is a reiterated summary of the lessons at the end of the book for ready reference. The application will be different in every case; if you are embarking on your 'leadership' journey you may wish to read through the lot, if you are looking for a specific reminder, then the notes you have made will bring you quickly back to the story or illustration.

I recognise the experiences that I have drawn on are very specific to my life of learning but I believe they will apply to other experiences. I think best way to ensure the learning or development is appropriate is to develop your own stories. The lessons can apply to those in small and medium businesses, charities, social enterprises, departments within large corporations and to those in the military. By reflecting on these illustrations I hope people can use them as a springboard and avoid some of the pitfalls and hazards that we all face in our daily business.

Always Start With a Very Clear End-state

Strategy

Start with the end in view

If you are not clear about where you are going, or where you wish to be, then you will not be able to focus or prioritise in order to achieve a long-term aim.

Your horizon will close in and while you may feel you are working hard, you will not make progress towards the ultimate goal. Your efforts will shift from one urgent issue to the next; you will have the sense of being busy, without the satisfaction of progress.

The idea of 'Mission Command' is central to all military planning and execution. Great effort is put into making sure the whole team is clear about what needs to be achieved – the end-state.

The 'end-state' describes where we want to be when the action or activity is complete. This could be a range of things and might be brought about by parallel activities that are political, economic or social as well as military.

Mission Command gives freedom to commanders at subordinate levels to develop their own plans to achieve the required aim.

I recall a presentation for a job in the NHS where I showed a slide about the need to be accurate with words when describing the end-state. One needs to be very clear about *what* needs to be achieved, very clear about *when* it should be done, but not so rigid on the *how* there should be freedom for your team to develop their plans.

General George S. Patton said, 'Never tell people how to do things. Tell them what to do and they will surprise you with their ingenuity'. Pay and promotion might inspire some but the greatest incentive is when you are able to use your own initiative.

As the lead logistic staff officer in the Enabling Command part of the Allied Rapid Reaction Corps, a UK-led NATO Headquarters, I recall numerous exercises where we practised our ability to write plans and contingency plans. The old adage 'no plan survives contact with the enemy' rings true in all walks of life. As soon as a plan is written, it is time to start work on the 'what-ifs' and on some exercises we prepared six or seven variations to the original document. I have seen frustration generated in the Army and the NHS when operational delivery has not strictly followed the original plan. I am not suggesting plans should be ignored or treated lightly, but being prepared for the various 'branches' of the original makes for a more robust planning approach. There is an element of 'anticipating the unexpected' that can be done and then planning for that contingency can reduce the subsequent impact, remove the likelihood of surprises and ensure one remains in control should the 'unexpected' actually occur.

When conducting any planning process be very clear about what you are asking to be done, or what is being asked of you. Scrutinise the words in the mission and make sure you properly understand what is required; seek clarity when uncertain. I recall in my final term at school, in a three hour exam, I had been furiously writing for over an hour when I realised that I had misread the question. I had ignored the advice to take time to 'read the question' and was so eager to gain a good grade that I started writing almost as soon as the papers were turned over and I caught sight of a question I had revised. A few minutes to recover my composure and then less than two hours to write the answer to the actual question. The result, I passed, but only just and with more stress than necessary and learning a very important lesson in a painful way.

A plan will require specific resources, time and overall approach. Consider the military mission to seize a hill. If the mission was to hold, secure, deny, or occupy the hill the plan would be subtly or significantly different. When looking at a task given, or preparing one for your team, be very clear about what is to be achieved.

General George S. Patton has also been quoted as saying:

'A good battle plan that you act on today can be better than a perfect one tomorrow'.

I was reminded of this when, as a captain on an important career course, I had to complete what is called a Tactical Overlay. Essentially this is a trace that can be laid over a map, showing in graphical form the concept of an operation. Details are contained in short text, with the deployment of friendly and enemy troops, the scheme of manoeuvre and key timings all shown in a pictorial format.

The Directing Staff (DS) called me in after the exam: 'this is the neatest, clearest and best presented tactical overlay I have ever seen … however it is unfinished'. He continued: 'it is of no use to your troops as it does not tell them exactly what they have to do'.

I was awarded zero points. A whole term, hours of work, complete application, dedication and commitment to learn the details and present my work in the best possible light and my score was zero.

A scribble on the page that showed the whole plan would have scored more. I accept that sometimes the goal becomes more focused as you proceed along the journey and indeed that there are times that the end-state needs to be revised and I am not suggesting a rigid adherence to the original vision should things change along the way. However, the painful, but fundamental lesson I learned that day was to always start with a very clear understanding of what you are being asked to do.

Lesson One Summary – Start with the end in view

In practice this means that you must give clear direction, ensure your team know precisely what you want to achieve and then give them the freedom to deliver.

There are five key principles:

1. *Describe the end-state*. This is a challenge with projects and change programmes that often start without a clear understanding of where they are going. In the creative arts world this may well be of value, but in any form of business, describing the objective of the project in clear terms will allow the progress towards it to be measured and more easily corrected if it veers off course.
2. *Don't constrain ideas* at the conceptual stage; but once the mission is written be clear that is exactly what you want to be achieved.
3. *Use Mission Command*. Once the mission is determined, support the initiatives and ideas of your teams; they may find different ways of delivering what you have described. They are closer to the delivery than you are, so give them the freedom to shape their own route so long as it leads to your destination and meets the timeline.
4. *Resist the temptation to delve into the detail*. It erodes trust and confidence and far from conveying to your troops that you have an understanding of the job they do, it suggests you think you could do it better!
5. *Read the question*! Little more to say, but make sure you are very clear about what you need people to do.

Lesson Two

When to be a Leader

Leadership is a full time job

Recognise that leadership is something one does through behaviour and actions rather than something 'just for work'.

More than this, good leadership encourages leadership in 'followers' and by investing time in those you lead, they in turn, can become leaders themselves.

Simon Sinek in his book *Leaders Eat Last* quotes a US Marine Corps General, Lieutenant General George Flynn who says that 'the cost of leadership is self-interest'. The leader has to consider the needs of those he or she leads ahead of their own personal requirements.

We all have our favourite leaders; when we think about leaders we often think of heroic people, those we have heard or read about. I look to General Gerald Templer in Malaya (and his 'hearts and minds' campaign), a soldier I studied when working on my promotion exams; and also to Field Marshal Bernard Montgomery who commanded 3 Division in the Second World War, a Headquarters in which I subsequently served as Commander Logistic Support in 2006.

Other leaders come to mind in the NHS: Elizabeth Garett Anderson and Nye Bevan are certainly good examples and their names have been used for the key leadership programmes run by the NHS Leadership Academy. There will be inspirational leaders for those working in other sectors but I suspect anyone with an interest in leadership will be able to quote a remark or two from their favourites.

It is my view however, that we are all leaders, wherever we may sit in an organisation, when it comes to personal example. Leading is a full time business and it is not easy. What you write and what you say may be carefully thought through to inspire and motivate your troops; but what you do and how you do it, your behaviour, is also part of setting the example.

Leadership works 'both ways' too. Things you do will be noticed; if you turn up late for meetings, do not read the meeting paperwork in advance, do not answer e-mails (or get distracted by them in meetings), then this set of behaviours will be deemed as acceptable by your team. They will do as you do.

First impressions

I remember reading about 'paradigm shifts' in the book by Stephen Covey (*The 7 habits of highly effective people*) where he describes travelling on the subway when a father boards the train with his unruly children. The man sits quietly with his eyes closed while the children shout at each other and upset the rest of the carriage. Stephen Covey eventually asks if the man could control his children and he explains that he has just come from the hospital where his wife, their mother died; he is not sure what to do and he thinks they are not sure how to behave either. Stephen relates how in an instant his understanding changed from irritation to sympathy.

I recall one evening at my swimming club a young girl joined my lane and after the coach had explained what we were to do, we needed to decide who should lead off. She now had her back to me and I said that I was happy if she took the lead but before I had finished speaking and without saying anything to me she just set off. My ego a little bruised I swam after her thinking it a bit rude that she did not even acknowledge my comment. When we got to the end of that part of the session she stood up and faced me and I had to strain to understand her as she explained, slowly, that she was deaf! My assumption that she had rudely ignored me shifted immediately to one of understanding and a desire to help. The old adage, 'you never get a second chance to create a first impression' comes to mind and I suggest that 'example' is not something you can go back and set; you have to deliver all the time.

Early lessons

My early experience of leadership was rather brutal. On arrival at the Apprentice College as a sixteen year old I was introduced to Army discipline. Each floor of our accommodation block housed 24 apprentices in four man rooms with three apprentice Corporals each sleeping in a single room, looking after two of the four-man rooms. The apprenticeship lasted 2 years and those in their second year played a part in organising, managing and educating the junior entrants. On this first day, my apprentice Corporal got the eight apprentices into the 'blanco' room (where we would later learn to clean our equipment) and stood in the middle of the group. He said that he was in charge, he would make decisions and tell us what to do and we would do it. If we did not we would get punished; the punishment was a punch in the stomach and he went round the room showing each of us what that would be like. With eight young people bent double, he left the room and it was clear to us that what he said we would do; leadership in action.

Example can be very compelling and I cite others throughout this book as having made an impression on me. I don't really blame the lad who was simply behaving the way he had learned from his apprentice Corporal. Having said that, blind acceptance of behaviour without applying your own values can lead down a very narrow road. It was clear to me that should I gain promotion, I would not use those tactics. We learn lessons both from positive and negative examples.

Reveille

The introduction to the Army morning call was not quite what I had expected either and provided another early leadership lesson. The gentle sound of a distant bugle call may have been in my mind, but reality was somewhat different. Each day at about 0530 hours we were woken by a duty apprentice banging a pick helve on the bannisters and shouting 'wake up' at the top of his voice. A pick helve is the wooden handle of large pickaxe used for digging trenches; as apprentices we were not armed and would patrol the barracks at night with a pick helve. The lad would come into each four-man room and 'toothpaste' us from our beds. The idea being that like a tube of toothpaste, we would be pressed from our beds by his action of smacking the pick on the bottom of the bed and then hitting further up the bed until we were sitting on the pillows or actually standing up. Reveille had been achieved.

Once again, imitating the behaviour of others without thinking through the consequences of the impact on your own values and standards is something I would not advocate. Unwise and indeed painful at the time, I decided one morning that I was no longer going to be forced from my bed in this manner and as the lights came on and the duty chap moved from bed to bed I decided I would make my stand. As he came to my bed, I looked him in the eye and did not move. His pick helve struck my shins and I continued my defiance by lying there looking at him. For a moment there was silence and then he moved on to the next bed. A small act but a significant episode in my time in the apprentice's college; the word would get around that I was not going to simply follow in the footsteps of my predecessors but make my own way, albeit hobbling for a few days with very sore shins.

I remember when I was an Adjutant preparing a discipline case for a soldier who had been reported for the crime of 'urinating in a public place' in down-town Aldershot on a Saturday night. The Commanding Officer admonished the soldier (essentially reprimanded but not punished); this was against the legal advice I had prepared with the military legal authorities that suggested this was a 'prevalent offence' and should attract the highest appropriate punishment. The Commanding Officer told me afterwards that this soldier had been on a sponsored walk and as CO he had joined them one afternoon; and while a field in the countryside may be different to a wall behind a pub, the CO was unable to prosecute the soldier for something he had, in effect, condoned by his own behaviour.

General David Morrison, when Chief of the Australian Army made a speech after an investigation into bullying in the Australian Defence Forces and during the talk he said 'the standards you walk past are the standards you accept' and I ask you to consider how many times have you walked past because it was easier than facing the challenge?

When accepting the accolade, the benefits and the status of being a leader in any sector or organisation we should also understand we accept the responsibility of being that leader all the time. I remember bumping into an officer in the NAAFI shop buying his newspaper on a Sunday morning. Unlike me, he had not shaved that morning, but he was in a public place and as an officer he ought to have set the example. Likewise, when at a Triathlon event as part of the Army team, I recall walking around the transition areas before the start early one morning and hearing the warrant officer in charge of our team explaining to a young lieutenant that as an officer it was his duty to set the example and that while it may be 0500 hours, 'If Colonel Pearce can shave before coming to this recce, so can you sir'. Later that morning, as we lined up for the start, the officer was clean shaven!

Ice Breaking Drills

Setting an example sometimes requires a conscious decision to do something.

During the Ski and Survival course in Norway there is an activity called 'ice breaking drills'. The idea is to prepare for a failure in the ice when crossing a frozen lake and there is a need for self-rescue. All soldiers serving in the Arctic Circle go through this preparation but there is an upper age limit due to the shock of sudden immersion in freezing water. The limit is only thirty-five and at the age of thirty-seven, I could have escaped the challenge. Being the Squadron commander however put me in a position where I felt I had a leadership role as well as wanting to know I could survive should the situation arise. The risk mitigation for the age is simply to have a medic standing by with a defibrillator. A hole is drilled into the ice, similar to a lane in a swimming pool. The test is to ski into the water one end, remove the skis and push them onto safe ice, remove the bergen and do likewise and then swim to the other end and use the ski poles to pull yourself onto more solid ice. An interesting aside is the fact that there is a rope tied to the bergen and to each of the skis to prevent them being lost should they slide under the ice, but no rope on the soldier!

The 10m Diving Board

When serving in Berlin I organised a series of military challenges as part of a monthly competition. Teams would arrive on a Wednesday afternoon having been informed only of the number of people required and the dress and equipment needed. Events included a long orienteering course with each team being taken by helicopter to the start point, so long as they directed the pilot to the right grid reference.

Another event required teams to negotiate a series of tunnels and then abseil from a high tower and another was an ice hockey competition which proved the value of all the protective gear you see professional teams wearing.

One event I recall was at the Olympic pool. The task was for a team of four, wearing military uniform, to jump from the 10m board and then swim four lengths, collecting equipment each end and by working together shifting the growing load to the finish. The thing my recce had not prepared me for was how far a 10m board is from the water. My team was the first to go and only when standing on the edge did I realise how I might feel in anticipation of such a drop. Leading by example, I had to step off with the lesson being that if you are going to ask soldiers to do something you must be prepared to do it yourself.

Be careful what you wish for

General John Wilsey, in his book about Lieutenant Colonel H. Jones Para[3], described the importance others put on what you say when in leadership positions. Being driven into the barracks one day he mentioned how shabby the doors on the vehicle garages were looking and then thought little more about it. Later that day, when being driven out of the barracks he saw a group of soldiers energetically painting the doors. The driver had mentioned the comment to the Regimental Sergeant Major (RSM), who took it as the 'commanders' intent' and immediately put painting garage doors at the top of the priority list.

> Walking around the Hospital one day with a member of the Board, I was surprised that on entering a ward there was a need for introductions. I had recently been around every ward discussing a new approach to conducting daily Board Rounds, so the member of staff recognised me, the new chap, but not the person who had been in the organisation for a number of years.

---

3   *H. Jones VC: The Life and Death of an Unusual Hero.* John Wilsey, Hutchinson, London, 2002.

Leadership is not just about heading the organisation, making critical decisions, attending Board Meetings; it is also about leading the people in the organisation, each and every one of them.

Zig Zigler made a pertinent comment which many quote:

'You don't build a business
– you build people –
and then people build the business.'

Another example of having confidence in the hierarchy was a time when I was under some pressure at home. I had been informed of a late change in my posting. Originally I was being posted to Berlin from the UK, so had to make all the domestic arrangements to prepare for the move. Very late in the day there was an indication that my posting may be changed and I asked for an interview with my boss, a Colonel. I prepared for the meeting by pulling together all the details of what I had prepared for my move and the impact of such a short notice change. When I went in to explain my difficult position, he started the conversation with 'Bob, you have come to talk about this sudden change of posting, you will have packed your house, arranged for storage for some of your belongings, sold your car, your wife will have given up her job and you will have made arrangements to visit schools for your children'. He clearly understood my position and I had not uttered a word. He said he would speak with the posting authority and sort the problem, which he did that day. When I got home I was interrogated as to whether I had read my list out to the Colonel and I explained I had not! In my defence, I said that somehow the Colonel seemed to have a copy of the list himself and knew my situation exactly. Empathy is a very important element of leadership and with a bit of thought and preparation, it is possible to gain a proper understanding of the challenges your team may be under. I would not advocate jumping to conclusions – much has been written about listening being a key element of communication – but I do recommend giving some preparatory thought to the conversation you are about to have.

This message is reinforced by Steven Covey in his book, *The 7 habits of highly effective people*. One of the key lessons is 'first understand then be understood'. The theory being we spend more of our time thinking about the next thing we are going to say than the thing the other person is saying. Have you ever had to say the words 'what did you say' during a conversation when you have been internally distracted by thinking of when you did something similar to what the person is describing to you? Another example in the book is about jumping too quickly to conclusions before the speaker has finished. The example is when the manager in a shop overhears a customer being told by the salesperson, 'no, not had that for a long time and don't expect it anytime soon'. The manger rushes in to say how he was sure they would be able to arrange for a delivery, but then realises that they had been discussing the weather and the lack of rain recently!

Engage the Troops

General David Richards when Commander in Chief used to walk through the Headquarters on his way to the office. Clearly he was a busy man, and the walkabouts favoured by senior officers were difficult to programme into the diary. His way round the problem was take a different route through the large Headquarters building each day on his way to work. He would bump into people and have a brief chat about what they were doing. The walkabout does wonders for morale and the impact of the CinC talking to someone about their work was a great boost to them – and their team – and would be discussed for some time afterwards.

When Brigadier Arthur Denaro[4] was Chief of Staff in the Headquarters in Cyprus, he would walk around at the end of the day to ask what you were doing. He was clearly a senior officer and initially it was a surprise to find him wandering the corridors but had a relaxed and engaging way of getting the best from his team. The impact was not to encourage us to stay late on the off-chance he wandered into the

---

4   Later Major General.

office, but the opposite as he would often ask what it was you were doing and why was it so important you were working late!

Another example comes from my time in 3 (UK) Division. The General Officer Commanding (GOC) was Major General Lamb[5] and this incident happened one morning as I arrived for work. Walking towards the Headquarters, the General's car drove by and out he got, wearing a leather jacket over his uniform as a precaution to being obviously military when on the roads. As he walked through the front door there was a young soldier looking slightly lost. The soldier saw this person and asked 'do you know where the Engineers' Department is mate?' Now I have known many senior officers who might have responded in various ways but General Lamb said, 'sure, it's this way' and led him down a corridor. He then returned to go up the stairs to his office. A very small gesture but a reflection of the man and his values. Is it what we would have done, do we always have time for other people?

It is not only senior officers who teach lessons. I was a major in Cyprus when a young Royal Navy Lieutenant was posted into the Branch and worked for me. I remember walking into his office one Monday morning and launching into the urgent work of the day, with much to do and some sharp deadlines.

He looked up at me from his desk and calmly replied, 'Good morning, how was your weekend?' It took me by surprise and I recognised the blurring of the urgent and important lines in that short moment. As a leader I felt the pressure of the workload and had taken my eye off the fact that I needed to lead people, not just deliver outcomes.

Dwight D. Eisenhower is reported to have said 'I have two kinds of problems: the urgent and the important. The urgent are not important,

---

5   Later Lieutenant General Sir Graeme Lamb KBE, CMG, DSO.

and the important are never urgent'. One needs to remember that those working in your team have more in their life than just the piece of work you need them for and trying to understand their pressures will help you get the most from them.

Group Think

As a newly promoted Lieutenant Colonel I found myself in the Corps Planning Group (CPG) on a major exercise with the Allied Rapid Reaction Corps. My role was to contribute the logistics input to the planning process.

The room was filled with the 'warrior types' from each Nation, contributing to the development of the final action of the exercise, the decisive attack on the red forces. The lead was a British full Colonel who had a fearsome reputation and did not gain multi-national agreement by consensus but simply by demanding it and chewing up anyone who disagreed.

The plan was coming together and standing on a table in the middle of the room he asked for comments from the 'back seats' (where the logisticians, medics and other support staff sat). There was silence for a few moments and then I put my hand up.

'What' he blasted! And standing up I proceeded to challenge the time he had set for 'H' Hour (the time the Division would cross the line of departure to commence the attack). I explained that the 'pass time'[6] of the Division travelling from the current position, on the number of routes selected and considering the distance to be travelled, would mean the Division would not be in the forming up positions until well after the stipulated H Hour. Unless we identify additional routes, or start the move earlier, H Hour would have to be delayed.

There was silence in the room. The Colonel was either processing the information or about to sacrifice another officer and banish me from the CPG forever. After what seemed an age he quietly said to his 'scribe' (the chap taking notes as the wargame progressed), 'delay

---

6   The time it takes for the whole convoy to pass a given point on the route (first vehicle starts the time, last vehicle stops it).

H Hour'. Then he looked directly at me and said 'get your logistic calculator out and let me know the very earliest we can launch the attack'. I had made it, I was part of the team and I scooped up my spreadsheets and trotted out to refine my calculations.

The lesson was clear, if you are to challenge the growing energy behind a direction of travel, be very confident in your position; do your homework, do the number crunching, know your business and have the confidence to speak up when you sense things are getting out of hand.

Take the lead

Attending a Quality, Service Improvement and Redesign (QSIR) course organised by the Gloucestershire Clinical Commissioning Group (CCG) based on the NHS Advancing Change and Transformation (ACT) Academy approach, I was surprised by one of the exercises. We were asked look at the posters on the wall showing elements of the QSIR curriculum and stand by the one we were most comfortable with. The curriculum includes leadership, project management, demand and capacity, sustainability and a few others. The majority of the course were standing by the Engaging and Understanding Others poster, with some, by the Measurement for Improvement and a group (from the Project Management Office) standing by the Project Management poster. I was the only one standing by the Leading Improvement poster. We were on a programme looking at delivering change and on the module titled Leading Improvement and only one person in a room of 34 was comfortable with leading improvement. There was a very clear lesson on day one of that course about why change in the NHS is difficult to implement.

Write it down

One way of ensuring your message gets through is to write it down. Even when deployed on operations it can be useful to write down your thoughts or views to make things clear to those you command. I wrote some letters to my officers while deployed in the Kuwait desert in 2003. The situation in Iraq had developed towards the end of 2002 and early in 2003 my Regiment was deployed to Kuwait as part of the UK contribution to Operation Iraqi Freedom as the Americans called it. In a series of four letters[7] written to my officers during the deployment to the Iraq War I reinforced my thoughts on leadership. The first was in February, titled 'Commanding Officer's Intent'. Having deployed early in January the letter set the store for the coming few months. I talked about the importance of setting a personal example and communicating with the troops. The second was on Risk, as we

---

7   Transcripts of the four letters can be found at the end of the book.

were in a warfighting scenario, something many had trained for but few had actually experienced. The letter explained the first phase, the deployment had been completed and we were now under pressure to deliver all the vehicles, fuel, ammunition, stores, food and spares for the UK forward troops. I quoted an extract from the Army publication on Operations: 'A commander should accept the inevitability of confusion and disorder' and stressed that it was their job to take calculated risks based on military judgement. The third letter was titled 'The Middle Game' and addressed the uncertainty of having initially deployed in a concentrated manner we were now moving into a period of 'sustainment' where we need to continue to provide a high level of support to the deployed forces. In the letter I recognise that soldiers and officers will be tired and frustrated at times, but that is exactly when leaders need to be at their best. The fourth letter was written in May as we started to plan for our return to Germany. This letter encouraged the officers to maintain their focus, particularly as soldiers started to think of going home and reminded them to have safety uppermost in their minds.

Lesson Two Summary – Leadership is a full time job

There are many definitions of leadership. One, from one of our greatest military leaders, Field Marshal Bill Slim, is this:

'Leadership is simply yourself'

Leadership is how you are and what you do. There are five things that I have learned:

1. *Everything you do will be noticed by your team*. You cannot change what you are but you can be conscious of how you go about your business and how you are perceived by your staff. Walking into head office, sitting at your big desk for the day and walking out will convey a message, but not necessarily the one you wish. Occasionally turning up unexpectedly at the desk or office of members of your team and asking what they are doing will convey a very different message

about how you value their contribution.

2. *Set time aside in your diary to talk with members of your team.* Your diary often runs your life and meetings fill the time; book slots for engaging with your team. If they are in the diary they are more likely to happen, but they must be seen as important as other appointments or they will easily be shifted or replaced with other 'more important' events.

3. *Put yourself in the shoes of the person you are about to engage with, interview, talk with....* Listen to their concerns to confirm your assessment, but do the preparation – value them as whole people rather than employees.

4. *If you are in a leadership position, take it seriously,* it is a full time role. It is important to understand the needs of those you lead; put them before your own.

5. *Do your homework* and have the confidence to say your piece and take the lead.

6. *Be prepared to modify your decisions* in light of good evidence.

Be the leader you would want to lead you

Lesson Three

Teamwork

You can't climb a 12-foot wall on your own

The value of teamwork is fundamental to all military activity and is equally transferable to many other sectors. While we talk of the importance of leadership, tasks are rarely completed by leaders alone.

Engaged, empowered and motivated team members who understand the end-state will deliver an output greater than the 'sum of the parts'.

How to climb a 12-foot wall

One of the first memories I have after joining the Army as a sixteen-year-old apprentice was the assault course competition. We were divided into small teams and I was determined that my team would be the fastest over the obstacles and make a good impression so early in our Army careers.

Setting off I led our team and was flying over the obstacles feeling some early confidence that we were going to do well. Suddenly I came to the 12-foot wall. It became clear to me, very quickly, that I could not get over the wall on my own; I needed somebody to help.

I waited for the next lad to join me and heaved him up and did the same with the next. The last two remained on the top, stretching their arms down; I launched myself up as they caught my arms and pulled me over the wall.

This lesson has stayed with me throughout my career; while teams need leading, leaders also need teams; the coherence of the whole group can achieve great things.

In the NHS I have seen a number of 12-foot walls. I suggest that meeting the four hour target, often seen as an ED problem is only solved by the whole hospital (indeed the whole healthcare system) playing a part in delivering the solution.

Looking to the future, implementing the Five Year Forward View (5YFV), integrating health and social care through the Better Care Fund, or changing the way services are delivered through some of the integrated models in the Sustainability and Transformation Plans are also 12-foot walls that need whole-system teamwork in order to climb over.

Interlocking Arcs

I remember at Sandhurst digging a trench on Salisbury Plain, one of the first exercises and one where your hands are wrecked, blistered and bruised from trying to dig a 6 foot trench into hard chalk. Part of the business of setting out the Platoon area is that each trench can provide 'interlocking arcs of fire' essentially the extent to which a soldier in the trench can fire to the left or right. The importance of this is clear, there are no gaps in the fire cover that can be provided across the frontage of the position; so long as those in the other trenches are alert, their weapons are clean and prepared for firing. There is a real sense that in a trench you are part of a team that can bring an impact greater than the sum of the parts, by working coherently together.

Understand the message

I recall having a coffee at about 1700hrs with a Consultant when his telephone rang. It was a ward sister, asking him to come to the ward to review some diagnostic results for a patient. When the call finished I asked if he needed to go and he said not immediately. He explained that he had seen the patient early that morning, had asked for some tests to be conducted but had then done an appraisal with a junior doctor and some other activities, including meeting with me. Busy and tired, he had forgotten to go back and see the patient. The fact that the hospital was in dire need of beds and that the bed management team was trying to find the right beds for the patients queuing in the Emergency Department was not a pressure he felt in his ward doing his rounds.

The role of leaders is not to have people do the right thing only when they are standing over them, but to inspire and encourage people to do the right thing at all times. We should not judge the behaviour demonstrated by the consultant without checking how he would get up to date knowledge about the flow status in the hospital. Fundamentally, inspiring people to do the right thing should be a 'force multiplier'[8] and spread the good practice across the whole organisation.

---

8   A capability that, when added to and employed by a combat force, significantly increases the combat potential of that force and thus enhances the probability of successful mission accomplishment.

The slowest man

At the age of thirty-seven as a Major in the Army I found myself on the All Arms Commando Course; trying to earn the coveted Green Beret. The prize is so well respected that I recall later, when deployed in Iraq in 2003, I turned up at a Royal Marines' base in the desert wearing my body armour and helmet, to be greeted by Royal Marines wearing berets; they needed nothing more to protect them!

> Back to the commando course; a gruelling twelve week course of physical and mental tests, designed to wear you down and reveal sometimes to yourself as well as the Directing Staff your strengths and weaknesses. There is a series of marching tests; wearing a seriously heavy bergen (rucksack) and marching at a pretty fast pace. The march simulates moving to an objective where some other form of military action is to take place; a means to an end. The tests are to be completed as a squad and clearly when marching as a squad, you can only march as fast as the slowest man. There is often frustration when individuals find it hard to keep up, but if you sacrifice your slowest man, you will then march … as fast as your slowest man, as well as being a man down.
>
> Indeed, if you keep doing this then you will not be able to get over the 12-foot wall at the end of the march!

The lesson is to make sure every member of the team is properly prepared, doing the job they are best suited to and contributing to the success of the team. We don't always work with people we like, but we should recognise the skills and value each member of the team brings to the overall outcome.

'If a man does his best, what else is there?'
General George S. Patton

In the NHS all too often I have seen people blamed for poor performance. To me, poor performance is often a symptom of a poorly performing team, which means the team need to look inwards and work out how to improve, not kick out the 'slowest' man and then be looking around nervously at who might be the next slowest.

We should have pride in and loyalty to the organisations we work for; like the Royal Marines. We should consider the impact of sacrificing the slowest man; the impact on that person and the longer term impact on the morale and ability of the team.

Value the team

I think it is important to recognise the value of your team; there is always a risk that leaders believe that the success of the team is solely down to their leadership. I have often reflected on the notion that when one is working with a strong team, then there is a willingness amongst all to do things 'for the team' rather than for personal interest. While I don't really know (and that is the whole point) I am certainly aware that I have not always done everything right when leading my teams, but strong teams have anticipated, decided or just done things which have supported the overall intent, even if I have neglected to instruct, communicate or deliver the direction. The strength is twofold: in the team that is willing to work in such an altruistic manner, and in the humbleness of the leader to know that, if they are sitting on top of the pyramid, then there is a lot of support below, much of which is unseen.

In a speech at the University of Houston in Texas[9], Arnold Schwarzenegger highlighted this fundamental aspect of leadership by stating 'I always tell people that you can call me anything that you want. You can call me Arnold. You can call me Schwarzenegger. You can call me the Austrian oak. You can call me Schwarzy. You can call me Arnie. But don't ever, ever call me the self-made man.' His speech gave examples of the various achievements throughout his life, from body-builder, to actor and now as a Governor in the United States. He reinforces the fact that we all need support by going on to say: 'and the

9   Arnold Schwarzenegger – 'None of us can make it alone', 12 May 2017, University of Houston, Texas, USA.

reason why I want you to understand that is because as soon as you understand that you are here because of a lot of help, then you also understand that now is time to help others. That's what this is all about. You got to help others. Don't just think about yourself. Help others.'

He 'Aint Heavy, He's My Brother[10]

One of the early lessons on the Commando Course was the importance of what is known as the buddy-buddy system. It exists in the Army and I remember my first introduction was in the 'gas chamber' when we were testing our respirators. During the process, when the chamber is filled with CS gas, part of the test is to remove the canister that filters the air, and exchange it with another soldier. The idea is to replicate the process of replacing your canister due to damage or the length of time exposed to a 'dirty environment'. Standing opposite your buddy, who also helped put the hood up on your protective 'NBC' suit, you remove each other's canister, pass them behind your back and then exchange them.

The buddy-buddy approach is taken to the next level in the Royal Marines; there is no place for an individual, the team is prime and your efforts and energy should always be directed at supporting the team effort.

On the Commando Course all students are treated the same; regardless of rank. I was a Major at the time and thirty-seven years old, not the normal fit, young soldier. The youngest on the course I recall was only seventeen. Having said that, the group quickly learns to work together, with the regular speed-march training and the significant challenges of the various exercises. I recall one where we had to dig trenches in pairs on the common and live in them for a week. Not a particular challenge you may think, but it was winter and of course, wet. Indeed the adage, 'it's not training unless it's raining' really did apply. A completed trench is about 6 feet deep, together with a sleeping trench stepped up a couple of feet and covered over the top. The bottom

---

10   The Hollies, 1969.

of the trench had filled with water which came up and over our boots. We took turns on sentry and for some not very convincing reason, our sleeping bags had been replaced with blankets. Imagine sleeping in a muddy trench, wrapped only in a blanket and during the periods of darkness, with no lights or cooking. After living in this hole for a couple of nights I woke for my turn on sentry, shivering and getting cramp in my legs. I stood up in the water, teeth chattering and the other chap, a Lance Corporal, climbed into the sleeping trench. He was moving around a lot and eventually reached out with a mug of steaming hot chocolate he had prepared during daylight and kept until the early hours in a vacuum flask; he had decided my need was greater and offered to share his drink. It was the most welcome boost to my morale, much greater than its intrinsic value and the sort of act many in the Armed forces will be able to recall. Properly looking out for each other is the fundamental bedrock of effective teamwork.

When one member of our course failed the speed-march and shoot test because his weapon would not fire, he had to re-run it the next day. The remainder of us were shattered and wanted some well-earned rest; but a small group joined him for the re-run. We had nothing to prove, but we were not going to leave him to the mercy of the Directing Staff without any support from the rest of us. It reminded me of the comment earlier on the course, even the strongest on the team may need to rely on the skills of others at some time; we all need someone to watch our back.

The Army uses the phrase 'Jack' when somebody does something for themselves. The 'I'm all right Jack' approach is alien to the military. If you make a brew for yourself and not for the others in the team, it will be referred to as a 'Jack brew' and you will feel guilty as you drink it!

Talking with a Reserve Sergeant one day about a deployment to Sierra Leone with a medical detachment he explained that while he was very much a specialist, the whole hospital was aware of the situation it faced at all times; a collective approach to the delivery of their mission. A separate discussion with a senior military nurse reinforced this collective approach.

She explained that when deployed to a military hospital there was no sense of 'going off duty' if another nurse was busy, there was a sense of collective responsibility. I acknowledge that the nurse in Iraq and indeed the chap in Sierra Leone were both without any other distractions or call on their time; they did not have to shop, pick up the children or indeed do anything other than rest and then come back on duty. However, the sense of collective support was strong, and the idea of leaving a comrade to struggle because your duty period was finished was alien; these people pulled together to deliver a successful output.

There is a story of Christopher Wren, one of the greatest of English architects, who walked one day unrecognised among the men who were at work upon the building of St Paul's Cathedral in London which he had designed. When he inquired of one of the workmen what he was doing, the man replied, 'I am cutting a piece of stone'. He put the same question to another man, and he replied, 'I am earning five shillings two pence a day'. A third man answered, 'I am helping Sir Christopher Wren build a beautiful cathedral'. That man had vision. He could see beyond the cutting of the stone, beyond the earning of his daily wage, to the creation of a work of art.

Leaders should ensure their teams understand the importance of the Main Effort and that each member plays a key part in delivering a successful overall outcome.

Lesson Three Summary – You can't climb a 12-foot wall on your own

You may not be climbing walls or marching with heavy packs but getting your team to pull together is as important to your business as it is in any other organisation. The collective power of a well-oiled team is so much greater than the sum of the parts and the responsibility of the leader is to inspire the team:

1. *Work as a team, you will achieve great things*. Understand the value of the team; remember you can't climb a 12-foot wall on your own.
2. *Value the team you have.* The team will operate at the speed of the slowest person, but everyone has skills that may be needed at some point. Sacrifice your team members at your peril, you may be losing valuable skills and you may create an atmosphere of scepticism and mistrust.
3. *Treat your team with respect.* Engender a sense of support, encourage people to move from silo working, through good communication and understanding of their part in the overall output.
4. *Every member to contribute.* Hold the team to account; clearly there are times when individuals are rightly responsible and that has its place, but where possible, congratulate teams for their collective action.
5. *Leaders need teams and teams need leaders.* Recognise that you cannot do everything on your own. Ensure every member of the team understands the Main Effort.

'None of us is as strong as all of us'[11]

---

11   Sir Clive Woodward, *Winning*. Hodder & Stoughton, 2005.

Trust and Reliability

> ### We all need a sentry to guard us when we sleep
>
> However fit, however strong, all of us, including leaders need to sleep. We can only sleep if we have confidence in those around us. Clearly this applies to military operations, but the concept is applicable to other sectors.
>
> Trust, in those you work with, needs to be earned both 'up and down' the ranks.
>
> When you know your back is covered, you can focus fully on the challenges ahead.

Cover my back

The idea of the man at the back of the patrol 'having your back' is second nature to military people. I recall talking to my daughter about having made an arrangement to meet a friend in some months' time and she suggested as we neared the date that I should confirm the arrangements. I said that unless he told me the meeting was not on, I need not confirm; I duly drove to the RV on the date, and met him on time.

Trust

In his book, *The 21 Irrefutable Laws of Leadership*, John Maxwell explores his sixth law of leadership – the Law of Solid Ground. He offers the premise that trust is the Foundation of Leadership. Leaders build trust by consistently exemplifying competence, connection and character; violate the law of Solid Ground and you diminish your influence as a leader.

Andrew St George, in his book *The Royal Navy way of Leadership* states the importance of trust and soft skills:

'People thrive on autonomy, trust and responsibility – the fruits of a soft skills ethos.'

Trust is something you earn rather than get just by having a role of responsibility or leadership.

As a young Lieutenant I had organised some training on Dartmoor and was keen to meet the troops out on the hill. Having driven as close as we could, we then had to walk to the checkpoint. 'Follow me' I said to the two soldiers with me and marched off across the bog. The next moment I was almost submerged, with my legs kicking but finding nothing to stand on and the only thing stopping me going further down was my rucksack stuck against the side of the hole.

I shouted for help needing the others to pull me out. The shout back was shrouded in laughter as they pointed out that I had the rope on the back of my pack!

As the leader, I had the rope, the map, the responsibility but not the experience. Clearly, not all my lessons have been learned from positive experiences and being eager to lead from the front when not really sure of your ground is a fundamental lesson. I may have had character and connection, but at that stage I clearly did not have competence.

Similarly, when working on a time sensitive project in the NHS Trust which required a number of General Managers to provide input to a document I was compiling, I set a tight deadline for their contributions. I had to chase a couple and was disappointed that I had to check up on a General Manager who was an ex Royal Marine. I then found my mobile phone was playing up and having re-set it discovered a message from that manager, the night before the deadline, explaining he would be about 30 minutes late with his input and the reason for the delay. He had done exactly as I had expected of a military man and informed me before the deadline of the potential delay.

Rest

Margaret Thatcher and Churchill famously needed only a few hours' sleep each night but soldiers recognise the importance of rest and recuperation. I recall on the All Arms Commando Course living the adage that if you were not working, then you should be cleaning your weapon, eating or sleeping.

The importance of rest, particularly for the leader, should not be underestimated. I remember at the end of a long three month deployment to Norway, on one of the last days having completed all my duties and really just waiting for the redeployment flights I took time out to go on a ski tour up a local mountain that I had seen throughout my time on the exercise. I skied to a point where I could sit down and made myself a cup of tea; I was alone, the view was tremendous and I was able to reflect in complete tranquillity. I can still draw on the absolute peace and quiet I found on the mountainside that day when in times of high pressure and anxiety.

When on exercise or operations, living in the field as it is called, soldiers can only rest and sort out their admin (cook, clean weapons and equipment) if someone else is on sentry duty. The responsibility that goes with the sentry duty is significant, if you cannot rely completely on the person on sentry, you cannot switch your focus to other things and certainly not sleep. During the Arctic Survival Course in Norway we had to dig a team snow hole and survive the night. Once inside, we would light a candle and take it in turns to be on 'candle watch'. The sentry keeps an eye on possible enemy activity but also on the 'sinking' of the snow hole as the roof lowers with the effect of the body heat and of course to ensure there is a flow of oxygen; a critical role in support of the team.

Another example of trust comes from a story told to me by a Warrant Officer who had recently left the Army. He had moved to a large organisation and on day one, was shown to his desk. He was then taken on a short tour of the office by his line manager and when he got back his wallet was missing. His boss asked where he had put his wallet and he explained that he had left his wallet and car keys on the desk before they walked away on the short tour. The boss said it was his own fault that he had lost his wallet, leaving it out like that! The Warrant Officer thanked him for his time and left the job that day; if he could not trust others in the same office, he was clearly not in a place where he could work.

On the All Arms Commando Course I recall a particular time when we had to display confidence and trust in others. We were on Dartmoor and at the top of a cliff face ready to 'forward' abseil. Essentially this requires you to run over the edge of the cliff and rely completely on the man in control of the rope. Literally putting your life in the hands of another engenders a real bond and prepares soldiers for what they might face when deployed on operations. The value of what the Armed Forces term Adventurous Training cannot be underestimated; having to make decisions, trust others and explore personal limits is all part of developing young leaders.

The annual Remembrance Sunday event, recognised since the First World War, brings to the minds of many, those who have given their lives in what is often called the ultimate sacrifice. The bond that brings military people together is born from their commitment to lay down their lives, no doubt in the heat of the moment more for their 'brothers in arms' than any higher cause. Nevertheless, when leaving the military, many find the lack of a similar commitment in other walks of life difficult to understand. While I am convinced of the strength gained from a group of soldiers bound by this commitment, I believe that leaders can

instil at least an element of collective gain being greater than the individual reward in other walks of life.

Having had a conversation with my General Managers in the Hospital about this idea I remember going to one of the daily 'Bed Management Meetings' when the hospital was in a challenging position and we needed to improve flow. There was a problem with the cardiology service and the General Manager for cardiology was not available. Rather than people shuffling their feet and looking at the floor, ignoring the request, the General Manager for Gastroenterology put her hand up and said she would take the task. I was impressed, not only with her willingness to take responsibility for something within the Medicine Division (and clearly not her area), but also with the fact that she made nothing of it, simply resolved the problem and carried on with the rest of her own job. A great example of supporting others and taking on responsibility in order to 'get the job done'.

I was in a meeting when a discussion revealed that there was a major event being hosted by the Trust in two days. The task had not been given to anyone to run and organise. There was a moment of silence. The Improvement Director who had been parachuted into the organisation to help address our shortcomings asked who was leading. I put my hand up.

Her aim had been to identify a gap in communication, but I had closed that opportunity by stating that I was leading. I then raced around on the day to organise the event. Not our best effort, but clearly avoided the potential embarrassment as we had invited a number of people from outside the organisation to assist. It later transpired that the Improvement Director had *known* the event was not organised and asked in public at the meeting in order to expose where the organisational chain had broken. I had readily volunteered (and she had subsequently assisted in delivering the event); so she had not achieved her aim of flushing out the communications problem! I did not feel happy that such an error was to be exposed in public, because my sense of 'team' was strong and I was willing to put myself in the position of responsibility rather than expose failings in our team. One can debate the action but I was not prepared to allow the public embarrassment of a team member and preferred to address the shortcoming privately.

After a long and tiring Command Post Exercise (CPX) (a headquarters deployed in the field but no troops on the ground) with the Allied Rapid Reaction Corps we were called into a large theatre for the 'hot de-brief'. The American Brigadier General was at the front with a microphone, highlighting key lessons. At one point he mentioned the importance of keeping the commander informed and asked me to stand up. He said 'did you inform the commander of the fuel contamination at 0200hrs on Tuesday morning?' Clearly, I had not, but I had directed an immediate test of other fuel holdings to be conducted, isolated where the contamination was and directed that fuel was not to be used.

I tried to explain this to him and he asked the very same question again; 'did you inform the commander of the fuel contamination at 0200hrs on Tuesday morning?' Again, I was about to defend my thinking when I realised what he was trying to illustrate. It was important to understand, that even in the early hours of the morning, there were times that the commander should be told of the situation. He had chosen this example and I was not supporting the line. I said loudly, 'no sir I did not inform him' and he was then able to go on and stress this valuable lesson.

Commanders' Critical Information Requirements (CCIR). This is an approach used when we are developing a plan, sometimes adapted to ensure that the team understand what it is the Commander should know and when. I remember using the approach when on an exercise with the Allied Rapid Reaction Corps, discussing the circumstances that would mean we should wake the Commander of the Enabling Command. We also discussed the approach in the Hospital when considering at what stage a duty manager would inform the duty Director and when the Chief Executive himself needed to be called. In the school, we had the same debate about the need to inform the Headmistress of various incidents. Clearly an accident involving pupils would mean we would inform her, but what about an inquiry from the media about some form of allegation in the school? It is by working through the examples that we can ensure that those on duty, often on their own, are able to make the right decisions for the team.

'Failure to plan is planning to fail' is often accredited to Benjamin Franklin. The Improvement Director in the NHS Trust used to say 'hope is not a plan' whenever she heard us use the word 'hope' when briefing her about the details of an improvement project. In the NHS a new Chief Executive explained that she was not happy with a lack of progress on some of the improvement programmes. She also acknowledged that some people had slipped into presenting plans that met the need despite having little confidence to deliver them as stated. What she wanted from people was realistic plans; if the deadline set or the target measure was too challenging, she was to be informed of a realistic one. Having said that, she stated very clearly she would then expect you to deliver to the realistic target and hold you firmly to account; but that was a fair deal I thought.

A Good Quartermaster

Be prepared! On a recce to Kuwait in early 2003 I found myself standing in the middle of the desert being told 'this is where your Regiment will be'. I saw little but sand in all directions.

Then suddenly, driving towards us, lights flashing and horn beeping was a 4 wheel drive vehicle, part of our recce team. It was clearly warning us of a potential Chemical Weapon attack; we grabbed our respirators to mask up and take shelter in our vehicle. One member of the team had left his respirator in the accommodation. If this was real, he was going to suffer, or die from the potential attack and we were all looking at him as we struggled to pull our own respirators on.

The Quartermaster calmly reached into his daysack and pulled out a spare respirator and handed it to him.

I know that Quartermasters have a reputation for pulling 'rabbits out of hats' but this was truly amazing. When we deployed on the recce we all had a baggage allowance and had just managed to squeeze our helmets and respirators into our bags; he had taken spare kit! Not only that, on the morning that one of the team had forgotten to take his respirator, this QM had taken both his own and a spare! Lessons include thinking ahead as well as thinking about the other members of your team – oh, and always have a reliable Quartermaster!

Would you step forward for your team?

Lesson Four Summary – We all need a sentry to guard us when we sleep

Aristotle uses the Greek word *hexis* to denote moral virtue which has often been interpreted to mean habit. He suggests *hexis* is more than virtue, however, it is an active condition, so we are what we habitually do. Leaders need to be conscious that everything they do is seen as an expression of their character and an endorsement of their standards.

1. *Be true to yourself.* If you have said you will do something, deliver it or tell someone you will not deliver it – before the deadline.
2. *Be confident in your work.* Produce realistic plans and deliver to them; don't provide the answer that is being looked for without the confidence to deliver.
3. *Show confidence in your team.* Trust your people. One person cannot do everything; we all need a sentry to guard us while we sleep. Demonstrate confidence in your team, step off the cliff when they have the rope.
4. *Plan and prepare.* No plan survives contact with the enemy, but it is just irresponsible not to have a plan.

Lesson Five

Decision Making

Stand still right or wrong

Have the 'courage of your convictions' based on good research, sound planning and strong personal values. Don't be stubborn in the face of a changing situation, but be prepared to stand your ground and be counted when you sense you are right.

'The matter of "decision" is vital. The modern tendency is to avoid taking decisions, and to procrastinate in the hope that things will come out all right in the wash.' General Bernard Montgomery.

There is much in the academic literature on the difference between leadership and management. In commercial terms there appears to be a separation between the leader who sets the strategy, vision, future direction and motivation and the manager who delivers through thorough planning and the application of protocol and process.

I would argue that in the modern world they are more interlinked nowadays, people look to their managers, not just to assign them a task, but also to inspire with a sense of purpose. A Brigadier I worked with in the ARRC used to say:

> 'You cannot lead without an understanding of how your intent is going to be translated into action.'

I suggest that having a practical understanding of what you are asking people to do is fundamental to success. When I took command of 7 Transport Regiment I issued a letter explaining my Intent to all my officers; how I would conduct operations and what I expected of them[12]. I explained that in my second week in command I wanted to thank them all for an excellent handover and then went on to state my approach for the Regiment:

A highly professional unit ready for operations, in which soldiers and families enjoy serving.

The letter then had a series of sub paragraphs explaining my approach with regard to the professionalism of individuals, particularly the commanders, my thoughts on learning from mistakes and the importance of readiness to deploy. There was a section on teamwork and leadership and responsibility and then some words on communication, discipline and the place of the family and diversity in the unit. Safety, fitness and efficiency also featured, with a summary stating that I was a strong supporter of mission command; that individuals will make decisions based on the overall intent and in line with their own personal standards.

I did a similar thing when taking over as Director of Operations in the Medicine Division in Gloucestershire Hospitals. This time a single page summarised my 'intent' and gave a clear indication of what my thoughts were on leadership and example[13].

Peter Drucker said 'what gets measured gets managed' and I have seen much of that in the NHS. Measuring progress through SPC (Statistical Process Control) and Run Charts and graphs without connecting the staff to the overall vision or aim. In my view, that is why so many of the initiatives fail to deliver sustainable change, because people are doing what they have been told, rather than being inspired to deliver the improved outcome.

---

12   A transcript of the letter can be found at the end of the book.

13   A copy of the note can be found at the back of the book.

Take time to assess

Before discussing the urgency and importance of decision making, it is important to ensure that you make decisions at the appropriate time. Sometimes it is prudent to take time to assess the situation before jumping in with a decision.

I remember talking with a Warrant Officer when I was the Officer Commanding of the Supply Squadron in the AMF(L). He was an 'ammo-tech' and had spent some time in Northern Ireland working with Bomb Disposal teams. One thing that wound him up was the habit of his officers, when a crisis struck, to stop and 'make a cup of tea' which in his mind was a way of stalling the immediate action that needed to take place. While I agree that there are times when urgent action is necessary and indeed in some instances there is no need for 'thinking time' I feel that the few minutes taken to assess a situation is often time well spent. Indeed, an opportunity to canvass opinion and talk with your team, before you make a decision is often well worth the time.

A paramedic friend of mine tells me that he is no use to a casualty if he has become one too. When I was commanding my Regiment and there was a need for some decision making with the Adjutant and Regimental Sergeant Major we would have tea and custard creams. It was a real surprise and a welcome break when deployed in Kuwait, in the middle of a desert and sitting down to do some serious planning for the war, that 'by magic' the Adjutant produced custard creams!

Make a decision

Making decisions is one of the most fundamental aspects of being a leader but we so often find we are not making progress for want of a decision. I think the first example in my mind comes from when I was an apprentice having just joined the Army at the age of sixteen. We seemed to spend most of our time on the Drill Square learning to march up and down, stand up straight and move as a squad. The lesson was to do with making mistakes when an order was barked out at us. The Drill Instructor used the phrase; 'stand still right or wrong' and it stays with me.

When the drill order is shouted out, you move in a precise manner; so 'shun' brings you to attention from the 'at ease' position. If you get it wrong, and everybody else has come to attention and you have not quite got your feet together by the end of the movement, when everyone else is rock solid still, you try to slide your feet closer together you will be spotted! The learning is that you should make a decision, be clear about it and stick with it. Don't let things slip after the decision.

I find this is true in the health service, where evidence is rightly the foundation of decision-making and doing things without reliable evidence might be considered reckless. But there are times when the desire for evidence slows the process down. Indeed, there may even be scope to make a decision and get some action while simultaneously seeking further evidence. In one meeting I suggested we get on with something which everyone in the room intuitively thought was right, but the decision was that we should spend another week or so confirming the evidence before we took action.

Making decisions and conveying them clearly is a key leadership quality. Too often in the NHS I have noticed a lack of progress due to an absence of clear decision making or indeed conflicting activities occurring due to a lack of clarity. In one small example a discussion at a morning meeting about the option of closing a ward became muddled when no decision was made. There were two approaches: either move patients from a few wards where beds were free and close a ward, or ensure patients were not spread across whole wards by concentrating them together to make the nursing tasks easier. The complication was that due to the time of year, the empty beds were not going to be long lived and we would have to open a closed ward again in a few days' time. The Nursing Director made a good case for simply reorganising the empty beds to one end of each ward as opening and closing a ward brought a whole raft of other infection control issues. Without a decision at the meeting however, confusion set in and at a routine management meeting some two hours later, it was discovered that both options were in the process of being implemented.

The challenge of providing proof or evidence and then judging the value of that evidence is not new of course. Tales of the fictional character Baron Münchausen pulling himself from the mire by his own hair was reviewed more recently in a *McKinsey Quarterly* article about behavioural approaches and the challenge of trying to quantify the benefits of processes that can 'de-bias' strategic decisions. Essentially, they discuss the regressive argument of 'each proof needing a further proof' with the resulting stagnation in decision making being the only result.

There are times when decisive action is necessary. I recall having to remove a senior soldier from an organisation with little notice. Something he considered humorous was not seen in the same light by others and had an impact much wider than he had intended. Action was required to prevent further fallout. My decision was immediate and very clear. Some of the hardest decisions are those that impact on peoples' lives and sometimes the decisions one has to take are difficult but when it comes to it, as Drucker famously summarised:

> 'Management is doing things right, leadership is doing the right things.'

Decide for others

Sometimes people need the leader to make a decision for them. I recall being deployed in Kuwait as we prepared for the crossing into Iraq. I had a message from home to explain that the wife of one of my soldiers had been taken into hospital and was about to miscarry. He had not informed me and while we had handed our mobile phones in for security reasons, we still had intermittent communications with home. I called the warrant officer to my Headquarters, explained I was aware of his situation and he explained his thinking; that if she did miscarry he would ask to go and support her but his job was here as we were about to go to war. I said that it was now that his wife needed his support and he was to pack his bags and leave that very afternoon. He returned before we launched into the offensive operations but needed someone else to make the decision which he ought to have made. Sometimes you need to ask yourself what advice would you give to someone else when these difficult decisions need to be made.

Just before we deployed I was also involved in a discussion about a married couple serving in the unit, with a very young child. We had received a formal notice to deploy. Essentially the unit was 'warned for operations' and I explained that the benefit they had of both serving in the same unit was also a risk if we were to deploy; both of them were essential to the delivery of our outputs and I needed both of them to deploy. They arranged for her mother to fly out to Germany (and be registered as living in the married quarter and responsible for the child) and all was well. Clearly I felt for the challenge of both parents deploying to war and the risk that entails, the choice had been theirs and it was not fair on others if they had received special treatment. I was content to make the decision as I believed it was the right thing to do. Having said that, there was no suggestion from either of them that they should be treated differently and both deployed and were professional to the core.

I have noticed that decisions seem to take longer to make and longer to implement in the NHS than in the Army but it is not immediately apparent why this should be the case. Decisions to change specialist services, shift the bed balance in a hospital from Surgery to Medicine or to employ additional staff in order to deliver an improved service all seem to take an age. In the operating theatre a surgeon will have a clear impetus to make decisions but in the management arena there is often a need to seek further data, further evidence, to ensure the decision is the right one rather than to defer to the experience and judgement of the decision maker. There is a balance required here. Sometimes delay is a positive thing, but essentially an assessment of the time a decision is needed is a good starting point.

In the Army I have worked on many plans and one of the key start points is plotting out *when* the decisions need to be made. A campaign plan has a series of Decision Points which relate to a point in time or a series of contributory factors that will require a decision. I believe that in any sector, to make progress we need to start by putting some effort into designing the Campaign Plan, identifying when decisions need to be made and the criteria that drive them. Setting out the approach like this can help avoid some of the paralysis that many organisations suffer from with regard to decision making.

I recall working in the Army Headquarters in Wilton during the Kosovo Campaign. While the early planning was being conducted I was responsible for the timeline for the production and distribution of body armour. The UK did not have sufficient body armour, or rather, lacked the ceramic plates to go into the over-jackets; we had to purchase more from specialist providers. Working backwards from the likely deployment date, I produced a timeline and a paper explaining the impact of delays. The decision date arrived. For a variety of reasons, not least the fact that openly buying body armour would declare our intent to deploy before any political debate, no decision was made. I continued pressing for a decision within the Army Headquarters but we did not have the authority without political agreement. I made alternative plans to fast track the delivery and distribution but subsequent 'critical' dates also passed without a decision. In the end, when the decision was made, we had to rush the equipment to the organisations already deploying and the impression given to the troops was not only one of incompetence but also of carelessness – that the organisation did not value people in the way that they ought. Neither of these things was true, but the impression given was not good and did not give confidence to the troops.

Decisions with insufficient evidence

The Pareto rule is used in many guises, but essentially suggests that 80% of the effects come from 20% of the causes. 'Perfect is the enemy of the good' is attributed to Voltaire, and I recall General David Richards making a similar statement when I was serving in the Allied Rapid Reaction Corps in Germany. As Chief of Staff, in order to generate and maintain momentum, he would state that 'excellence is the enemy of the good enough'. Preparing plans and contingency plans required a sense of urgency and he ensured we maintained a balanced perspective.

Having deployed at short notice to America as part of a three-man team to plan for the UK intervention into Afghanistan in 2002 I was living out of my suitcase but managed to go for a run around the barracks. While out running I was bitten by an insect; the bite swelled up over the next two days; and I could not do my boot up. As we had deployed as the immediate reaction team, we had no detailed medical documents, just a small summary card. I went to the US medical officer on our team who explained that without documents I could not be seen by their system. A senior Special Forces doctor on the planning team, however, had a different approach, initially holding a large bayonet and suggesting he could sort things out … but then getting me admitted to the medical centre for treatment.

I have often been in circumstances in the Army when a decision needs to be made and one does not have all the evidence one would wish. The US Army calls these VUCA situations (volatility, uncertainty, complexity and ambiguity). At such times judgement, comes into play; if a decision needs to be made, then it has to be made with the evidence available. Delaying the decision can be the least desirable option but can often be the one people take while wanting more evidence. In the Health Service there is a huge appetite for evidence-based decisions and rightly so, but a surgeon in an operating theatre faced with something unexpected does not stop to wait for an academic paper; he or she makes a decision there and then and stands by it.

Sometimes a timely decision is far better than a late one.

Don't get backed into a corner

I recall being briefed when on the Commando Course about the importance of the Emergency Rendezvous (ERV). When out on patrol, it is important to nominate an ERV should something unexpected take place. If the patrol is disturbed or distracted and has to split up, then each individual knows where they should go back and meet up with the others. This agile approach is something military personnel are very familiar with and being able to deal with the unexpected is an important lesson that transfers to other sectors. When giving orders for the patrol, the commander will specify a number of 'actions on' activities to ensure that there is an alternative option available whatever happens during the event. Actions on ambush, actions on vehicles approaching, actions on completion of each phase of the patrol, the list goes on but the fundamental principle is to think through what might happen and what options are open, before the issue becomes immediate.

Much later, when deployed to Kuwait at the start of the Iraq War in early 2003 I remember my Regimental Sergeant Major (RSM) coming into my tent to discuss a problem with one of the TA soldiers in the REME Workshop. He had joined the Regiment on deployment from a Reserve unit and it had been reported to the Workshop Sergeant Major that he had a 'tongue-stud' which contravened our standing orders as a potential hygiene and health and safety concern. The Sergeant Major had called the soldier in and ordered him to remove his tongue-stud but the soldier had refused. The Sergeant Major had spoken with the RSM who had, in turn ordered the soldier to remove it and again, he had refused. The RSM came to see me to ask me to order the soldier to remove the stud. My reflection was that the game the soldier was playing would go beyond me as he continued to 'refuse to soldier' as the formal charge would be called. As we were preparing for war we did not need people refusing to soldier. I said I would not see him, but had already made a decision; he should be put on the next flight back to the UK and I would write to his Commanding Officer explaining my disappointment in this young soldier and my reason for sending him home.

If you have the opportunity to consider the impact or implications of your actions then it is wise to think through the options and choose the best before they arise and you will avoid being backed into a corner.

Question Four

When conducting an 'estimate' as part of the Mission Command approach the Army refers to Question Four 'has the situation changed'. In the middle of a detailed analysis, it is important to stand back and assess the situation to make sure the plan you are developing is still relevant. I have often found myself in a 'question four' position where the situation has been pretty fluid and while my initial approach may be right, it is now time to reassess and think again. Just as being backed into a corner is to be avoided there is also a risk that having developed an intricate and detailed plan, you stick to it, despite the changing situation around you.

OODA(L) Loop

Colonel John Boyd of the US Air Force developed a strategy referred to as the OODA Loop. The concept was developed for his field of combat, air operations but has since been applied to other sectors. Essentially it refers to a decision cycle of Observe, Orient, Decide and Act which encapsulates the process we all go through to make decisions, be they in combat or in business. The art is to move through the process faster than others, indeed getting inside the enemy's OODA Loop is the way to achieve success. Added more recently is an L to the end to represent Lessons, reinforcing the importance of constantly assessing and reflecting in order to improve the next operation.

Lesson Five Summary – Stand still, right or wrong

*'You cannot escape the responsibility of
tomorrow by evading it today.'*

Abraham Lincoln

1. *Identify when or why decisions need to be made; and then make them!* Don't rush to decisions when taking time is appropriate, but don't put them off when a decision is needed.

2. *Follow through with your decisions; make sure they mean something to your team.* Hold people to account, when decisions are made, they should be supported by the whole team.

3. *Plan ahead; know when decisions are needed and support your team by making them.* Think through what advice you would give to others if facing the same challenge. Don't get backed into a corner. Consider Question Four.

4. *Spend time working out when a decision needs to be made.* Delaying a decision for a specific reason is acceptable, putting off decisions is not.

Resilience

Hold your nerve

Resilience is more than robustness under pressure; it is strength of character, born from your inner values and standards. The ability to remain calm under pressure comes from experience but you will already have a strong sense of 'right and wrong' and should gain strength from your own high standards.

'Whether you think you can or you think you can't, you're right.'

Henry Ford

When I joined the Royal Military Academy at Sandhurst I recall an incident which demonstrated a certain level of resilience, if not a little stubbornness.

Colour Sergeant Cox of the Coldstream Guards, our Platoon Sergeant, was at the front of the room. An impressive, shiny and shouty Sergeant who made a significant impression on all of us during our first term at Sandhurst. It was our first day and we had gathered in the classroom to learn how to bull our shoes! I was sitting towards the back and we all had to fill in our Regimental preference forms while making shiny circles on our toe-caps.

I had been in the Army Catering Corps as an Apprentice and been sponsored by the Corps into Sandhurst so I just wrote

'ACC' down on my sheet. Colour Sergeant Cox walked around collecting them in. I carried on working on my shoes and heard 'Where is Officer Cadet Pearce?' as he went on to ask 'you only have one choice here, what if the Catering Corps doesn't take you – you need a second choice?' with a wry smile on his face and to sniggers from others in the room.

I walked up to the front, collected my form, wrote on it and gave it back. As I was walking back to my seat he almost exploded as he read that should I not be good enough for the Army Catering Corps, my second choice was … the Coldstream Guards!

Not all difficult situations have been my own doing however. The Army approach to selecting officers for appointments is through a process managed by the Army Personnel Centre in Glasgow. Boards composed of senior officers with a broad understanding of the range of jobs they will be filling gather in the APC and review the individual files of those officers who have registered an interest in the position. 'Good morning, I'm the officer you didn't want' was my introductory remark to the Brigadier in the Allied Rapid Response Corps Headquarters as I walked into his office. Having been selected for promotion to Lieutenant Colonel I was posted to Germany. The role was G4 plans and essentially a logistic appointment, but it did not need a specialist logistic officer. The Brigadier (an infantry officer) had expressed his view in a letter to the APC saying he did not want a Royal Logistic Corps (RLC) officer in the post. The Board in Glasgow selected on merit and following my appointment, the Brigadier wrote a second letter requesting that the appointment should be 're-boarded'.

The Board, now back in their normal places of work, were sent the request and each member asked to reconsider the judgement. To a man, they stood by their original decision and I was duly sent to the job. By the end of the two-year tour, I had proved the Board right and my Brigadier was more than pleased with my performance and indeed I was graded top Lieutenant Colonel in the whole organisation, an unusual situation for a logistic officer!

Not long after returning from the Harvard element of the Executive Fast Track Programme, I was working on the development of a plan to move the NHS Trust to Seven Day Services and wanted to start a pilot in the Respiratory Service line. The planning suggested we would start on 1 October and things were being prepared but there were a number of hurdles to be cleared. Nearing the date, it became apparent that some of the obstacles had not been cleared and I was being pressed to delay the start date. We had already delayed by one month for good reasons but it became clear to me that further delay was almost inevitable due to the significant challenges of bringing about a change in the way of working.

I considered the situation and stated there would be no delay; the Pilot would start on 1 October. The Chief Executive asked me what he would see on 1 October and I said only a disappointment! However, once started, there would be a momentum generated and things would start to change. I felt it important to 'hold our nerve' and start the Pilot. We did just that and only a few days afterwards a manager came to me, explained that the Pilot had started, she would be asked for progress after the first month and wanted to engage to make sure progress was delivered. Others followed and we were soon on the first step of the journey towards delivering a consistent Seven Day Service in Respiratory.

The notion of building a plane in flight is something that Richard Branson applied when he initially set up his airline business. He reportedly sold tickets before he had an aircraft, used the money from the advance ticket sales to charter a plane and stuck a Virgin banner on the side. There is clearly a balance to be struck between recklessness and entrepreneurial spirit, but certainly there are times when it is important to *hold your nerve*.

Back to a story from my time as an apprentice, resilience is not always just a mental approach, but overcoming physical challenges can also require a dogged and determined attitude.

We were training on Dartmoor for the Ten Tors competition and there were two teams on the moor. The officer in charge was at the camp site where we would stay overnight and after a day of marching through the inevitable rain and fog I eventually led my team to the RV, later than planned but we were there. We set our tents up, cooked and ate our food and by midnight had our heads down, exhausted after a long march and ready to recharge for the challenge of the next day. About an hour later I was woken by the officer in charge because the other team had not arrived. Half of the team had walked off the moor to a road and called for transport to get them to the RV, but they did not have a grid reference for the remainder of the team and the reason they left was that one soldier had twisted his ankle badly and could not walk. The officer asked that I take another member of my team and try and help find the lost crew. I was shattered but knew the others would be in a bad way, particularly as the half team that arrived had half the equipment and did not leave those on the moor with a complete tent for shelter.

I explained to the officer that I would not venture back onto the moor with just one other man and woke my whole team. I explained the situation, we struck our tents and took all our equipment with us and set off into the mist. I retraced my route carefully by putting a man out front and guiding him onto the bearing before moving the remainder up to him. Slow progress with a tired team, but in a gap through the mist after what seemed hours, we spotted them. After helping with some hot drinks and sorting out their equipment, we slowly made our way back to the RV, once again set up our tents, and went back to sleep. Absolutely exhausted, but with a real task to complete and one of our friends injured out on the moor, we had set off to find them despite the impact on each of us; I was very proud of my team.

Resilience is not another word for being stubborn nor is it a defence when making decisions as the leader, but it is needed when things get tough and if you take on the responsibility of being a leader you must also be prepared for the challenges too.

Stay calm

Admiral William McRaven, the US Navy Seal, in his book *Make Your Bed*[14] says 'if you want to change the world, be your very best in the darkest moments'. He explains a significant challenge all US Navy Seal trainees have to complete, by swimming under a ship in the dark of night to place a mine. He goes on to explain that it is in these darkest moments that 'you need to be calm, very calm'. This collection of my stories cannot compare with the tales of such an esteemed military leader as Admiral McRaven, but I believe the lesson can be applied to leaders at any level and in any situation. Being able to detach from the danger, the chaos and calamity and carefully assess a situation requires training, confidence, resilience and inner calmness. Thinking clearly when others may be swept up in the commotion will set the leader apart and that leader may not be the most senior person present. There is something in the shared experiences that soldiers go through

14   Admiral William McRaven, *Make Your Bed: Little Things That Can Change Your Life…And Maybe the World.* Grand Central Publishing, 4 April 2017.

in their training and indeed on operations that enables them to manage crises and chaos with a calm and measured approach. I recall being in the middle of the Operations Room in the hospital during a particularly challenging night and one of the Band 7 nurses asked why I had not been shouting directions.

Her experience of some of the other people on duty during such challenging times was that the heat of the event spiralled upwards; but she observed I seemed to bring a sense of calm to the team. My reflection was that I had confidence that those working with me knew their jobs and my aim was to do my part (contacting the Executive on call, liaising with other Providers, particularly the Ambulance service) and not try and tell them how to do theirs.

Equally, there is the type of resilience needed to carry on when 'constantly knocked'. Once again, repeat training events have convinced me that the mental strength to drive forward is greater than any physical or indeed other barrier or hurdle. On the All Arms Commando Course we motivated ourselves with a song that was popular at the time being either played or indeed sung by the team which seems to have encapsulated the sentiment: it was called 'I get knocked down, but I get up again' by Chumbawamba.

Maintain a sense of humour

Another example from Sandhurst. We were on the Barossa Training Area behind the Royal Military Academy on a Saturday morning and were just coming back into the camp after about a 10 mile march. I was only eighteen and at the very start of my career as an officer in the Army but about to learn a very important lesson.

As we came down the hill with only about half a mile to go, the Colour Sergeant shouted out, 'did we enjoy that, gentlemen'? We responded with a somewhat lacklustre mumble of 'yes staff' but it clearly was not up to the mark. With that we were given the order 'about turn' on the march and in smart 'drill-square' fashion, turned round and were marching back up the hill towards the training area. We were sure that we would be asked the question again soon and would respond enthusiastically.

The trouble was, he did not ask us and we continued to march around the whole route we had just completed. It was not until we reached the halfway point that we were clear we would not be turning round and we ended up doing the whole march again; a total of about four hours out rather than two! On the way back into camp this time, in response to his question there was a resounding 'YES STAFF' response and we finished the march and the 'lesson of the day' with sore feet!

Be very much 'in the moment' to use the modern phrase and understand the importance of what you are doing at that time. Maintain a sense of perspective and humour helps to do that; if you have to march round again, do it well.

> 'Here is the prime condition of success: concentrate your energy, thought and capital exclusively upon the business in which you are engaged. Having begun on one line, resolve to fight it out on that line, to lead in it, adopt every improvement, have the best machinery, and know the most about it.'
>
> Andrew Carnegie

Down time

I think that the Army has a good approach to the business of 'letting off steam' or helping people to put perspective on things that have happened. The Royal Marines introduced Trauma Risk Management (TRiM) which is now used across the Services to help those who have been involved in traumatic events. The approach is to gather people immediately after a crisis or incident and allow them to talk through, with one of those present being a trained facilitator. This does not replace formal psychological support if it is needed, but is used during a respite in operational activity to help people through.

In the Health Service there are different levels of support, but the opportunity to stand back after a traumatic incident is rarely afforded due to the continual nature of the output. Linked to this is the fact that when deployed, the Army works as a strong 'band of brothers' where looking after each other is fundamental to successful soldiering. In a deployed environment there are no families, no hobbies, no distractions. Concentrated delivery of the work output is what consumes the mind the whole time. In the Health Service people go from work to home, do domestic and family duties, and have to cope with both work and the rest of life at the same time.

Lesson Six Summary – Hold your nerve

General Patton is quoted as saying:

> 'I don't measure a man's success by how high he climbs, but how high he bounces when he hits the bottom.'

I recall a Brigade Commander telling my wife at a dinner when I was a young Captain, 'he will go far, he can take a rollicking'. He had called me to his office that morning. The incident was one that I had not been directly responsible for, but the soldier responsible was under my command and I had accepted responsibility when he called me to account.

'None of us are born with it – it takes years of hard work and sacrifice to build. When everything's great, we wonder if we really need it, but when the going gets tough, we can't do without it.'

Richard Branson on Resilience

1. *Choose your moments*; don't confuse stubbornness with resilience.
2. Leadership is more than being in charge, it's about *having the mental and physical strength* to make decisions and stand by them.
3. *Be determined in seeing things through to a conclusion.* If you are made responsible for something then take control of how you will deliver it.
4. *Maintain a sense of humour.* Of the four elements of the Commando Spirit – Courage, Determination, Unselfishness and Cheerfulness in the face of adversity – the last is what gets people through the darkest moments. Maintain a sense of perspective.
5. *Know your team.* Recognise the challenges they face and the impact they may have on them; consider the whole person not just the element you see at work. Know them sufficiently well to notice behavioural changes.

Lesson Seven

Responsibilty

The cost of leadership is self-interest

Put your soldiers' needs before your own. It is a straightforward statement and something every young officer learns at Sandhurst. It applies to other walks of life too; if you are a leader, it is your responsibility to ensure your team is properly supported.

Don't blame the troops

Serving in the Army Apprentices College immediately after being commissioned I remember an incident when I arranged my first 'range day' for the platoon. It was my responsibility to produce an 'admin order' explaining when people needed to be where and with what equipment. I had considered the need for packed lunches but not designated anyone to order them; when I put in the formal request I was told it was too late and they needed 48 hours' notice. That evening I checked I had everything organised, weapons, ammunition, and transport but knew that I did not have the lunches. I drove to the local supermarket and bought 30 sandwiches, sausage rolls, crisps, fruit and drinks. An expensive lesson for a young officer but more than that, it taught me to have a little more understanding when applying the rules. My experience was the rule was there to ensure sufficient time to order the necessary elements of a packed meal; but if a request was late, we might still be able to do something! As a Catering Officer in 8 Regiment in Germany on my next posting I made a point that we would never turn away a request to feed troops. We sometimes had to follow up with the paperwork afterwards but it was not the fault of the troops and they should not lose out.

Jim Collins in his book *Good to Great* explains the characteristics of what he defines as level 5 leaders, those who can really take an organisation to 'great'. He stresses that when things go wrong, the level 5 leader will look to his or her own actions to review the problem; others look to apportion blame.

Following the death of one of my soldiers I recall being interviewed under caution by the military police. They suggested that I had contravened an order; my response was that if that was the case, then clearly I was responsible; so, what was the order? My solicitor did not think that was the right answer but I was in command of the organisation and therefore responsible for the lives of all the soldiers in it – if I had done something wrong I was ready to shoulder the responsibility. They presented the document to me and as I looked through I realised that I had not seen it before. I explained this and they looked at each other. It was clear that their evidence did not point to me. I was relieved not to be found responsible but equally, more than happy to take the responsibility should it have fallen on my shoulders. A salutary lesson to those who are tempted to roles of responsibility; while there may be benefits to enjoy, real responsibility should not be underestimated. Andrew St George in his book on the *Royal Navy Way of Leadership* refers to responsibility, authority and accountability; stating that there should be very clear lines for each team member and stressing the importance of accountability matching responsibility.

Not such a significant situation but another example is when, as a Commanding Officer, I was being driven to an appointment. My driver was driving too fast because I had been delayed getting into the car to go to a meeting at the Brigade Headquarters. She was trying to make up the time so I was not late for the meeting and I said to her that it was my fault I was late into the vehicle and therefore my fault I would be late getting out; her job was to get me there safely but not to make up for my failings!

The earlier reference to General George Flynn of the US Marine Corps, comes to mind again: 'the cost of leadership is self-interest'.

Have the courage of your conviction

During the Iraq War in 2003 I remember having to run to our trenches as the scud missile warning alarms sounded many times, night and day. One thing that stands out from that time was how sometimes we forget the way different events affect different people. Fear affects people in many ways and the macho environment of soldiers in a war is no place to show weakness.

> Having rushed from our sleep into our NBC protective clothing and respirators (it was much later that we discovered the enemy did not have weapons of mass destruction) we were once again in our trenches. I decided to walk around with my RSM and check the troops were okay. We came upon a commotion in a trench. One of the soldiers had been so racked with fear he had been sick in his respirator. The soldiers around him needed to know whether to take his mask off or to keep it on to protect him from the potential gas attack.

They needed someone to make the decision and I was able to make the call and get him cleaned up.

Own the problem

While deployed in the desert in Kuwait, with the Regiment working round the clock to deliver all the vehicles, ammunition and equipment up to the Brigade it became clear that we did not have enough people trained to operate the Rough Terrain Fork Lift Truck around the clock. We set up some training using the person most capable as the instructor; but he was not a trained instructor. At the end of some useful training he came to the HQ to say he was not able to certify people as competent as he was not accredited for that job. He was concerned and the issue was brought to my attention. I asked, 'have you trained these soldiers to the best of your ability to drive these vehicles safely?' 'Yes of course' he replied. I assured him that it was my responsibility for directing him to instruct them and I took full responsibility for their competence – he went off happy.

Another example from the same deployment to the Iraq War is the signing of 'driver's waivers'. This is the way that all drivers of heavy goods vehicles manage their work and rest time and it applies equally to the military. All our drivers maintain a 'driver's hours record' which shows how long they have been driving and how much rest they have been given. The rules do not apply in war. I decided that I would apply the same approach to extending the time my soldiers were expected to drive and so enforced the peacetime approach; in Phase One of the operations the Regiment drove over 550,000km and I signed over 4000 waivers presented to me by my Squadron Commanders to authorise soldiers to drive over sixteen hours a day. My thinking was that in order to ensure we selected the drivers appropriately for tasks we should be managing their hours. Likewise, when taking under command a 'squadron' of local water tankers which we needed to provide water to the Iraqi population in Um Qasr, just after combat operations had ceased, my REME Workshop Commander advised that the vehicles were not sufficiently roadworthy for our soldiers to drive.

The challenge was that I had to be content to allow local drivers to continue driving vehicles that we deemed unsafe. The decision was one of risk management; I would not let my soldiers drive the vehicles, the REME would do their very best to keep the vehicles safe and roadworthy and I would continue to 'let' the local drivers transport the water to the Iraqi people in their own vehicles.

Good and bad

When commanding a Squadron, the Regiment was subjected to a surprise fitness inspection. A team from the Division turned up to run a Battlefield Fitness Test for the whole organisation. We had to turn up at a certain time in the morning and do the test.

> My Squadron was late turning up and while we completed the test successfully the Commanding Officer was not happy; he wrote to me asking me to investigate and find the person responsible.
>
> While I knew what had gone wrong and who was actually responsible, I went straight to the CO's office and told him I did not need to investigate as I was responsible: I was the commander of the Squadron.

He accepted my line and it reinforced my approach to taking responsibility.

If you are in charge then make sure you are prepared to take the hit if things go wrong (and the credit if they go well too). Then make sure your teams operate to the standards you wish to maintain!

Live with the decisions you make

Discipline in the Army is something that sits within the chain of command and a remarkable amount of power is vested in officers at various levels. Non-commissioned officers also have an element of authority for minor demeanours, and while this process has to be controlled, there is much value in the process. I have certainly never taken this disciplinary responsibility lightly. The rules have changed slightly since I made a particular decision and I stand by the decisions I have made in this respect throughout my career.

On return from Iraq, an incident came to my attention: one of my soldiers was accused of sexually harassing a member of the civilian staff in the Regiment. The case file was particularly full and detailed; normally such serious allegations would be passed from the Regimental level to be investigated at the higher Brigade level. While there were some sections of the Army Act 1955 that I was not able to decide upon, I was able to dismiss all cases (this aspect has since been changed and serious cases can no longer be dismissed below Brigade level). In this instance, we had, in accordance with the Army regulations, sought military legal advice and the clear direction was to pass the case to Brigade.

My deciding not to pursue the case against the soldier accused of sexual harassment meant that there was no risk of the case simply being passed from one level to another with the result being a soldier on the 'sexual offenders' list for the rest of his life when it was clear to me that he had not committed the crime as accused.

The big lesson for me was to read thoroughly through all the detail and not jump to conclusions; while the summary of the case indicated the advice was simply to pass it on, a detailed reading of all the statements showed there was much more to it. So I challenged the initial legal advice and subsequently dismissed the case.

The lesson is twofold: first, have the courage of your convictions, the more so when you face a serious decision which will have an impact on someone, in this case for the rest of their life; and second, if you have a report or data, study it in detail before making your decision.

Be the leader

A Warrant Officer came into the office and told me there was a crisis and I needed to do something. It was a very early tour in my career and I wondered if I was about to be drummed out of the Army. I asked him to explain; once he had, I made a decision and he went off to do it. I relaxed a little until a month or so later the same thing happened. It was clear to me that I had a responsibility and his way of operating was to follow the clear direction from his officer. I was initially surprised that one so long serving in the Army needed guidance from me as quite a junior officer at the time, but then realised that it was indeed my role to make these decisions.

Similarly, but much later, I was in a job where I saw a more senior officer avoid taking responsibility, feeling it was his predecessor's error that had caused the problem; he was not going to risk his career by getting involved. My position meant that I had responsibility but equally I felt it really was something that I should take on. It was over a very serious incident. I learned the lesson that the day you are given authority you must also take responsibility. There is no middle ground, no honeymoon period, leadership gives you responsibility and you should be ready to take it on if you want the leadership position.

Speak up ....when appropriate

I remember an incident when as Officer Commanding in a unit that was proud of its fitness we were completing the Combat Fitness Test (CFT). This is an 8 mile test (carrying a bergen) completed in different target times for the infantry and for logistic soldiers, the infantry test, obviously, being faster. Our unit worked to the infantry time and the CO was very pleased that he could demonstrate how fit we were. But on the day I remember, one of my soldiers collapsed on the run and was taken to hospital. After I had visited him, I decided I should speak with the CO. My Second in Command (2IC) advised against this action as he knew how proud the CO was of the unit fitness standard and how fierce he could be when challenged. My sense of responsibility to my soldiers was strong and I went to see him. I explained that he had left himself open to criticism, as a logistic unit we should be doing the logistic timings. Before he had time to react however, I also offered a potential solution. He could get us to do a timed march over the stated distance and afterwards declare it was the annual CFT which would have us do the event in the infantry time without stating that was what we were going to do in advance. He appreciated the discussion and that is how we ran things from then on.

When the sense of moral responsibility makes you feel like making a challenge, it is wise to think through the consequences and shape your approach. Make the challenge, but do so without creating confrontation, think through the options and offer a solution rather than appearing to simply disagree.

Take command

While serving in the Berlin Infantry Brigade we often went for a run in the mornings but this day the Physical Training Instructor (PTI) had set up a game of softball.

Being a bit of a runner I was sent to the far outfield. One enthusiastic soldier swung the bat wildly to hit the ball and then released it mid-flight to set off on his run. The bat struck the backstop on the head and he dropped to the ground, clutching his head, bleeding profusely.

From my position I saw almost the whole group of officers and soldiers rushing towards this poor soul but the thing that impressed me was the PTI who was calmly walking towards the growing crowd. As he arrived, the crowd parted and let him through, and as he went he was giving out instructions: 'contact the medical centre', 'go to the gym to get the first aid kit'. He was amongst a whole crowd of 'leaders' in various guises but was very much the person in charge and took control from the very moment that he did not join the group and rush to the point of crisis. It is so tempting to go to where the trouble is rather than solve the problem.

In a Divisional Headquarters on exercise often the busiest cell is 'G3 Current Operations' where the hour by hour tracking of the battle is displayed but resolving the whole campaign relies on the longer term plan and achieving the strategic goals. One can argue that the place to be is 'G5 Forward Plans' rather than observing the current battle.

In the Acute Trust where I have worked, the tendency when the Emergency Department (ED) is full to capacity was to go there – and to add to the chaos! I have made a point when on-call to go to the control room, not to the ED, and try and add value to the whole system rather than observing the point of crisis.

Recently, when studying the Governance model in the school it was pointed out to me by someone in the Health sector that when a Trust is in 'special measures' the NHS Improvement (NHSI) Regulator directs that a series of operational performance measures should be reviewed by every Board meeting. The question has to be whether directing the Board to look at current performance will resolve the situation or would time spent on developing strategic objectives do the trick?

The trappings of command

I have heard it said that upon our leaders we bestow great benefits and equally heard the criticism of those in 'privileged' positions not taking their roles seriously. A discussion with a colleague about leaders having to remain 'grounded' and not get carried away with the 'trappings of office' took me back to an exercise in Turkey when I was commanding my Squadron.

The Squadron Quarter Master Sergeant (SQMS) is responsible for all administrative arrangements and for this exercise, as we were to set up the Logistic Base in the far eastern reaches of Turkey in a completely green field site he was concerned about the amount of equipment we needed to pack. All facilities were to be arranged, water was shipped in tankers and bottles, food, fuel, ammunition and all accommodation arrangements had to be considered. Ablutions were to be set up 'in the field' and for our toilets he had a great idea. He had developed a space saving approach to the need to ship all our stores from the UK and had created 'four-man' latrines. These were wooden constructions that would fit over a hole in the ground (known as Deep Trench Latrines). Rather than building lots of individual toilets, he constructed fewer four-man units. The result, of course, was that when the situation called for it, you would go and sit next to a couple of other soldiers for your 'daily routine' – a great leveller for any aspiring leader.

Leadership is a serious matter however and it means taking decisions that have an impact on people. In the Army it can have the ultimate impact, the loss of life. Officers have to be conscious of the decisions they make and also think through what would happen following the death of a soldier. This subject is discussed at Sandhurst and something all officers are aware of, but not all of us have to actually do of course. In my time I found myself in this position a few times and they were the most testing times of my career. Meeting with parents to discuss the circumstances of the death of a child can never be an easy task and it is not something any officer takes lightly.

I also recall the time before my Regiment deployed to Kuwait for the war in Iraq. I went round to each Squadron to talk with the soldiers' families and brief them on situation as well as we knew it as I had returned from a recce to see the location where we would set up our logistic base. There were many questions about administrative arrangements and communications from theatre but one made me think very carefully. It was from a soldier's wife wanting to know what would happen to her husband's body should he be killed in theatre. The question was one of those in the minds of many, but one had the courage to ask it and actually, being able to discuss the process brought a small sense of relief all round. The point, however, was clear. We were not going to be on exercise, we were going to war and it was not certain that all of us would make it back. It is at these times the leader needs to be conscious of the trust and respect he feels he has 'earned' over years of command is actually a precious and valuable commodity. The soldiers and their families have complete confidence that the leader has their wellbeing at the forefront of his mind when making decisions and it brings home the meaning of the 'privilege of command'. Those who aspire to leadership positions need to understand that there may be 'trappings' but they go hand in hand with significant responsibility.

Lesson Seven Summary – The cost of leadership is self-interest

General Bill Slim famously gave this simple advice:

> *'I tell you as officers, that you will not eat,*
> *sleep, smoke, sit down, or lie down*
> *until your soldiers have had a chance to do these things.'*

1. *Accept authority and take responsibility from day one.* Do not pass blame for the shortcomings of your team. Jim Collins believes great leaders blend 'extreme personal humility with intense professional will'.
2. *Decisions made by your predecessor are now yours to own.* If you do not agree, change things, but don't hide behind decisions made by others.
3. *Use the evidence available.* If you have reference data, information or evidence, read it thoroughly before taking a decision.
4. *Speak up if you think something is wrong.* But don't just criticise, offer a solution. If you are going to question a decision, think through the options.
5. *Decide where you will have the best effect.* Being responsible does not necessarily mean go to the point of action; indeed taking the wider view may give you a better understanding of the overall situation.

Lesson Eight

Respect

Treat others as you would wish to be treated

Have your say, then support the decision of the leader even if the decision did not go your way. There is nothing more demoralising than a team being unravelled through insurrection in the ranks.

Respect

I was the Logistics planning officer in the Army Headquarters responsible for preparing the logistic support for a range of deployed operations. It was a fascinating job and one at the very centre of military planning for operations.

One weekend I was called into the office to prepare the logistic part of a re-deployment order for a small detachment in Africa. The logistic element was actually the major part of any redeployment so I was busy for much of the weekend; I issued the order and made arrangements for the troops and their equipment to recover back to the UK. On Monday morning, the G3 Ops Lieutenant Colonel was not happy that I had done all this from the logistic cell without G3 oversight. I readied myself for a dressing down when my boss, another Lieutenant Colonel, came into work.

Without stopping he walked through the office, I briefed him on the move, and he walked straight into the G3 Ops office to speak with the Lieutenant Colonel there. He told him that he had been kept informed throughout the weekend about the planning and had authorised me to send the order for redeployment!

> Trusting in your team works both ways, you should have trust and respect for your leaders but they in turn need to show trust in you. I had not informed my boss at all over the weekend, but he was ready to take the responsibility for one of his team, without question.

The Power of Empowerment

I recall doing a maths lesson at school about multiplication and the exponent, or 'to the power of' rules. The rule for the second power was called 'squared' or written as x2 and for the third power, called cubed was x3 for example. The thing that captured my imagination was the way an output seemed significant despite the relatively small multiplication factor. This arithmetical approach transferred in my mind to the world of Leadership and my sense was that outputs in an organisation could be vastly improved if the multiplication factor could be employed. The constraint in many organisations is the need to maintain control and we have all heard the statement 'but it won't be done to my standards' used when discussing delegation.

There has to be an element of self-awareness in recognising the constraining factor, but in my mind it is clear that I only have a certain amount of capacity. My capacity to make all decisions is constrained by my own ability or simply the time available. How many of us have been in a period of stagnation waiting for the 'decision maker' to come back to us?

I recall talking with the Chief Executive in the hospital about the size of his organisation; some 7500 people and an annual budget of around £450m. I asked how he could manage to keep on top of all the decisions, maintain the standards, just know what is going on? His response was quite telling; he said that clearly trying to make all the decisions that were needed would grind the organisation to a halt in quick time, so he had to 'empower' people to make the right decisions on his behalf. The way he did this was to put a great deal of time and effort into selecting his managers and decision makers. He personally interviewed every consultant candidate for example. In a school where I worked, the Headmistress personally interviewed every member of staff because every day they make decisions that affect the lives of the pupils in the school. Both said to me that selecting the right staff was the most important aspect of their role.

I have long believed that the output of any organisation can be multiplied 'to the power of' significantly if people are empowered. The contrary can be seen in many organisations too, where the boss works longer and longer hours, trying to keep hold of every decision. This approach can lead to a restriction in the development and progress of the organisation and also affect the health of the boss, eventually leading to poor decision making.

If I make the assumption that one person can spend eight hours making decisions in a day, then how different would the output be if say, ten people each had eight hours to make decisions? The challenge of course, is to find the balance, make the appropriate decisions at the top level and empower quality people to decide other things, resulting in a significant improvement in overall output.

Challenge

Blind allegiance or solidarity with your team is not always the best approach; sometimes there is a need to explore the proposed actions in a little more detail to ensure a sense of perspective is maintained.

Leading up to one November, preparations were being made for various Remembrance events, and units across Germany were being encouraged to run 5km for charity (cadet units and regular Army units). I was Commanding the Regiment and the idea was brought to me by my senior Physical Training Instructor. I agreed it was a really good idea but thought 5km a bit tame for a Regular Army unit. I suggested the theme of the event was about the number eleven; 1100hrs on the 11th day of the 11th month, so why don't we do 11 laps of 5kms? He and I talked about the logistics and off he went to make the arrangements. No sooner had he left the office than he was marched back in, flanked by my Adjutant and RSM. They had asked what we had discussed and came in to explain that there were not many in the Regiment who could march 55km! We had a discussion and I agreed

we would march out to the Ridge, do 11 laps of a shorter 3km route and the compromise was agreed. It was clear to me that it took some courage to come and tell the Commanding Officer that his plan was 'barking mad' but I was also conscious that I had to take heed of their advice.

After a very moving bugle call I quoted the Ode of Remembrance for the fallen before suggesting that as things got a little bit tough on the march with various aches, pains and blisters, my soldiers should consider what it was like for those in the trenches during the First World War. The event was indeed very challenging and not all completed the full distance in the time we had set but we achieved what I was after without getting too carried away. Respect is earned as a leader but it goes both ways and one should also enable and value questions from those working for you; if they have been bold enough to challenge then it is wise to consider their thoughts.

Chain of Command

In the Army I am used to working in a Chain of Command and respect is often assumed by one's position or rank. There is an inherent respect for those in the hierarchy within the Army but I have noticed a very different approach in the NHS and suspect it is equally relaxed or indeed absent in this form in other sectors.

Clearly respect has to be earned but there is still a hierarchy in any organisation. In the NHS I have been surprised at how some quite junior staff seem happy to criticise, complain, ignore or circumvent authority. A discussion with a Brigadier in the Army Medical Services after leaving the Army suggested a view that the responsibility for each doctor to make his or her decisions about patients and indeed be accountable for them makes, quite rightly, for an independent-minded workforce. This is not necessarily a bad thing and there is clearly a link between accountability and responsibility that all leaders must properly accept.

The challenge however, is that this independence of thought and action with regard to clinical decision making seems to have expanded into other aspects of the workings of a hospital or other health organisation. The result is a workforce that feels it right and appropriate to challenge any direction, be it related to clinical decision making or not. This in turn results in some areas where pockets of belligerent and confrontational relationships can work counter to the strong 'teamwork' approach seen in the military. The observation raised by the Medical Brigadier was in relation to a discussion about military medics; in his opinion they did not exhibit such challenge to the authority of the organisation and recognised the value of the hierarchy without it being in conflict with their individual clinical responsibilities.

Clearly there are times when soldiers simply need to act rather than challenge and discipline is part of the military ethos. I am not suggesting that the NHS should operate in the same way but there are times when the individual is not the focus and the team should take precedence. I have been quite surprised by the tone of some e-mails sent to Executive Board members and even directly to the Chief Executive from managers and clinicians. I sense that the perceived importance of the individual over the team is sometimes stronger in the NHS than in the Army where supporting the team is of prime importance.

I know best

Having said that, I recall sitting with my son, on the steps of his school, when he had to decide about his sixth form choices. We had a long discussion and he made a decision. Some years later, he reminded me of that discussion and the fact that he felt he had made the decision himself; I recall how difficult it was to avoid the 'if I were in your shoes' approach. He reflected that in his mind, I had always treated him as an adult and sometimes in work or other environments we impose our views rather than listen and allow decisions to be made by those who will then carry them out.

Priorities

When serving in Germany as a young Lieutenant, as the Specialist Catering Officer in a large Transport Regiment I made the most of the sporting opportunities. I became the officer in charge of the cross country team, the athletics team and the swimming team. I remember one day being under some pressure with athletics and swimming fixtures taking me away and I felt that my job was going to suffer. The Commanding Officer was particularly pleased with the success we were achieving on the sporting front, especially as we had not had our name in lights in the past and explained to me that my Main Effort was to win the Royal Corps of Transport Cup at the athletics meeting and then the British Army on the Rhine (BAOR) Swimming Championships in Berlin and he was not worried about the catering accounts!

There are times you will disagree with people over the decisions to be made or the direction to be taken. At these times, it is right to remember that their motivation is equally valid; don't assume people are trying to defeat your idea or are 'out to get you' but start with the assumption they are motivated by doing the right thing. I have sometimes found myself questioning a decision or a motive but have consoled myself with the understanding that the action or decision was based on sound judgement. Furthermore, and while this may not be an appropriate driver for behaviour, I am sure that like the Army, different sectors will have small circles of people and the chances are that sometime in the future you will meet up with people you have disagreed with in the past. My line is to be strong, represent your view but don't make enemies if at all possible. I am reminded of a quote from Richard Branson:

> *'Respect is how to treat everyone, not*
> *just those you want to impress.'*

One third/two thirds

How many times have you been conducting your planning, calculating your budget, setting out your annual objectives before you have received the information or direction you need to 'start' such work? The Army approach to planning is for the higher headquarters to ensure sufficient time is available for those receiving orders to develop their own plans. Very much part of the 'Mission Command' approach is respecting those you lead and ensuring they are properly resourced to do the tasks you are asking of them. The 'one third/two' thirds rule is mentioned in Army Doctrine Publications and briefed to all officers when they join Sandhurst. When receiving a task, assess the time available, take only one third of the time yourself and give two thirds of the time to your subordinate organisation to do their planning.

Sandhurst tea rooms

Respect comes from an inner belief that there is value in all people. I recall an early reflection of this when I joined Sandhurst at the tender age of eighteen. The daily programme was hectic and between various lessons we often had to change clothes to be ready for the next activity. A rare interval was when we sometimes snatched a break at the 'Sandhurst tea rooms'. We were able to buy a cup of tea and an iced bun and sit for a few minutes rest. One day as our squad dashed in for a break, the lady serving the tea responded to me by saying 'you always say thank you' which made me stop and think? With hundreds of officer cadets going through the tea rooms each day she found my politeness worthy of mention. Maybe being an officer and a gentleman was not something automatic for everyone and I would urge people to reflect on how they treat others.

John Adair in his book on *Action-Centred Leadership*[15] explains the importance of the relationship between the Task, the Team and the Individual. The completion of a practical task can be achieved by groups working together with shared goals. Success will follow if all members of the group work for the common good. However, each individual must be recognised and their needs met in order to ensure their motivation to achieve the group task. Successful leaders manage to balance these three elements. His approach to leadership is sometimes considered in conflict with the 'trait' leadership model that assumes leaders are born rather than developed over time. I sense there is a middle ground, where those with the right behavioural qualities can be taught the ways of leadership. My notion is that you need some of the basic behaviours in order to be recognised by your team as a good leader – honesty, humility, resilience for example – but through learning and application you can reinforce your leadership knowledge and practice.

Lesson Eight Summary – Treat others as you would wish to be treated

The Army Leadership Code[16] is founded on six key values: Courage, Discipline, Respect for Others, Integrity, Loyalty and Selfless

---

15   Adair, J.E. (1973). *Action-Centred Leadership*. McGraw-Hill, London.
16   *The Army Leadership Code*, First Edition, September 2015.

Commitment. The code states that 'Respect is a fundamental principle of the freedom that our society enjoys. Teams that embrace diversity, and value each individual for their contribution and viewpoint are always stronger for it. We must treat everyone we encounter, as we would wish to be treated.'

1. *Trust your team; they will trust you*. Demonstrate trust in your team; treat people as you would wish to be treated.
2. Don't underestimate the *power of empowerment*.
3. *Value challenge*. Listen and react to challenge from a member of your team in the way you would wish your boss to value your challenge.
4. *Apply the 'one third/two thirds' rule to planning.*
5. *Speak up,* but don't criticise without contributing to the delivery of a solution.

Lesson Nine

Be Prepared

Time spent in reconnaissance is seldom wasted

Preparation is everything! If you are about to interview somebody, have you set time aside to think about their issue? If you are commenting on some work prepared for you, have you set the appropriate time to read and consider it fully?

You show how you value your team and their efforts by the amount of personal commitment you put in to the exercise.

Be Prepared is well known as the motto of the Boy Scouts and something I grew up with as a scout and later reinforced during my time in the Army.

Mise en place

At sixteen, as an apprentice, I was learning from some great chefs in the Army which at the time had a renowned reputation for high class catering. The French term, *mise en place* means 'putting in place' or 'everything in its place'.

Essentially it refers to setting things up before cooking a meal; arranging all the ingredients, the utensils needed and preparing any food such as peeling vegetables, starting sauces and organising serving dishes. It has become much more than just how I prepare meals at home but a philosophy used to ensure I have thought things through before I embark on any activity or action.

As an apprentice, only sixteen or seventeen years old, I recall being called by the Sergeant Major and marched into the OC's office. I was

in my working dress and the OC ordered me to go and get changed
into my rig for ranges. I ran to my bunk and changed and ran back
up and presented myself to the Sergeant Major and he again marched
me into the office. The OC inspected me and then I was sent to get
changed into my Number 2 Dress (best uniform), which I did in double
quick time. On arriving back at the office this time I was inspected
then dismissed. It was some time later I learned that there had been a
discussion about whether to support my application for a commission
and my Sergeant Major had explained that not only was I turned out
well for inspections but my kit was always ready for any event. The
challenge from the Major was that if I was asked to go and get changed
right now would I turn up in poor order or would my other uniforms
all be ready for use. When I came in each time and was inspected
the OC had to concede that I had indeed got all my kit ready, my
boots cleaned and shined and was 'prepared' for the unexpected! I
am not sure how much this contributed but when I completed my
apprenticeship I did indeed go on to Sandhurst. The lesson was that

not only should you be prepared for what you know is coming, but always be prepared for the unexpected too; as best you can of course!

Not every experience was as positive however. I recall having to climb and shake the leaves from the trees when I was a young Apprentice. We had a Royal visitor coming to the barracks and very early that day the whole place was being cleaned. There were groups of soldiers everywhere and I was in a working party sent out to the grounds surrounding the drill square – to rake up the leaves. The corporal came over and saw there were some leaves on the grass where we had raked and we said it was because they had fallen after we had cleaned the area. So, to ensure no leaves fell during the visit we were sent up the trees to shake them. I remember this as it was very early in my Army career and I was impressed with the energy that was being put into the preparation of the barracks, even if I did feel a bit silly trying to prevent nature from doing its thing!

Later, when in Münster while serving with 8 Regiment RCT in the days of the Cold War the be prepared lesson was reinforced. Everyone in a Regiment of nearly 1000 soldiers had their kit packed in a bergen in the corner of their office, ready to deploy at a moment's notice. We regularly rehearsed the call out process (code name ACTIVE EDGE), sometimes parading on the Drill Square to be accounted for with the roll call and sometimes getting into our vehicles and deploying into the field. On one occasion we deployed for a week, with only the gear we had packed and prepared; that again taught the lesson that being prepared for the unexpected is a useful skill.

I think that experience has helped me develop a real focus on forward planning. I aim to be prepared for what I think will be coming up as well as what might happen if it does not quite go to plan. It prepares me for the unexpected and reduces the impact of last minute changes of direction.

An experience in the NHS Acute Trust reinforced the message when the Improvement Director explained that the numbers in 'unscheduled care' (the emergency patients that turn up at the A&E every day and night) should not be seen as a surprise but is largely predictable. Some detailed 'capacity and demand' work showed how we could predict the highs and lows of volume through the department and often the nature of some of the emergencies: children come in generally after school, elderly patients later in the day, particularly those referred by GPs after their visiting and referral process has taken place, and a range of other predictions can be made. Thinking ahead, aiming off, considering the 'what-ifs' are all elements of being prepared and the military saying 'time spent in reconnaissance is seldom wasted' rings very true with me.

However, there came a time when I had taken over as Adjutant and was keen to impress my Commanding Officer that I ought to have questioned the process. During the handover I was told that the morning routine was to take the Commanding Officer's in and out trays from his desk drawers and place them on top of the desk; putting them away at the end of the day. On my first day on my own, the CO came in and saw the trays on his desk and called me into the office. He asked why I had taken the trays out and why I thought he could not do it himself. When I explained that it was part of my handover he said that the previous Adjutant had been doing that for his own predecessor and the habit seemed to have carried on, but he did not need me to move his trays. Sometimes it is right to question the old habits or traditions!

Read the paperwork

Towards the tail end of my Army career I was invited to be the Senior Mentor at NATO School in Oberammergau for a Logistics course. The course is two weeks long for Majors or Lieutenant Colonels from all member nations about to take up senior logistic appointments in NATO Headquarters. The course is essentially about logistic planning and teaches the process through a range of scenarios; the candidates prepare briefing papers and verbal presentations. My role was to present an overview (by video conference) at the start of the course and then attend the second week as the senior officer they were briefing. This was hard work actually as the candidates deliver a series of very similar briefings and one has to pay attention to the detail and then de-brief the students and the directing staff at the end of each session.

The format for the opening presentation allowed each mentor to design their own talk to inspire the candidates. Mine focused on being engaged in the planning process from the beginning (in the past we would design the warfighting plan and then get the logistic staff to support it). I have always believed that engaging early meant that the warriors would design options supportable from the start, a much better way of doing business.

Then I said I would let them into a secret which had served me well throughout my career and would help them too. The secret would be shared just with this intimate group (about 100 people!) and they could use it as an advantage to help progress in their careers.

I spoke slowly and then said, this is the secret: when you are given something to read … read it!

Sounds very simple but I cannot count the times where I have been in a meeting discussing a subject with people who have not read the background papers. I remember a Brigadier telling me this 'secret' when I was a newly promoted Lieutenant Colonel and he said it had served him well too!

Value your work

I recall receiving a paper from an officer when I was Chief of Staff (COS) in a Divisional Headquarters. The officer worked for the Deputy Chief of Staff (DCOS) but this work was directly for me. I returned it saying that I was disappointed with her work and pointed out some of the errors in the annexes. Her comment was that she was surprised that I had read the annexes! I said if you give me something to read … I will read it! It reminded me of a comment from a General once when asked to sign something. The officer wanted the signature urgently and the General said to leave the document and he would read it and then sign it, saying, 'you may just need my signature, but I value it such that I want to know what I have signed'. Have pride in what you produce and make sure it meets your own high standards.

Write it down

Recently we said farewell to a key member of staff who had been in the Trust for twenty-seven years. Then another senior manager who had been here for a similar time retired and it made me think about the impact of such long service on the processes and procedures used in an organisation. Moving every two years or so in the Army meant that in every job there was a robust set of Standing Operating Procedures (SOPs) and a reliance on a good set of procedures and processes. In the NHS where people can stay in one organisation or indeed in one role for a long time there is little need to capture in writing the way of doing things and as a consequence many processes are not recorded. The value of having reliable and up to date SOPs does not need to be rehearsed, and in the Trust where I worked we embarked on a programme to capture good practice and record it in SOPs.

Contingency planning

General Eisenhower is remembered for saying 'Plans are worthless, but planning is everything' and he went on to say, 'There is a very great distinction because when you are planning for an emergency you must start with this one thing: the very definition of "emergency" is that it is unexpected, therefore it is not going to happen the way you are planning.'

General Stanley McChrystal when talking about his time commanding the Joint Special Operations Task Force in 2003 said about contingency planning 'I've never been on an operation that went as planned'.

I recall seeing a comment on 'LinkedIn' where some CEO was indicating that she felt that having a 'Plan B' was a sure way of saying she expected Plan A to fail. Her view was that a real focus on delivering Plan A was the way to success. I don't doubt the need for commitment and engagement to deliver a successful Plan A. However, I would argue that considering what might change, what elements of your early assessment may need to be revisited or which of your assumptions no longer apply are all valid questions. In the Army, the very first thing you do when you commit your reserve, is create another reserve!

My approach has always been to try and look beyond what you are expecting and think about what may happen. Then consider the options open to you should that manifest itself. One way to build confidence is not just to plan ahead but also to think through the 'actions on' as they call it in the Royal Marines and plan for those options too.

G3/G5

The Army refers to different branches by abbreviated titles. The G refers to an old General Staff term and the number reflects different cells in the headquarters. Most frequently used is G1 Administration, G2 for Intelligence, G3 Operations and G4 Logistics. Planning is G5 and there is a close relationship between G3 and G5. Indeed once plans are written, they are turned into operational orders by a more recent development, the G3/5 cell.

I had not been in the NHS all that long when I was asked to review the flow of patients through the hospital by the Chief Operating Officer. My approach was to determine in military terms where the activity was concentrated, and like many military organisations, the focus of effort was on the G3. The Emergency Department, the immediate need for people to move to in-patient wards and to be discharged from the hospital drew the greatest attention. The planning effort had little priority, few staff and was a weak area in comparison. My recommendation was to bolster the planning cell and thereby improve the longer term preparations for Bank Holiday staffing, incident management and the like. In any organisation there is a tendency to be drawn to the action rather than plan for the longer term. There is often a blurring of the operationally urgent and the strategically important.

In Army logistic terms, the G3 battle was no longer my concern, the ammunition, fuel and other stores had been delivered. My focus had to be on the next battle and how I could ensure the logistic support would be in the right place at the right time. In any business there has to be a balance between operational delivery and preparations for the future.

Digging a snow hole

Skiing back after a day ski touring on the Ski and Survival course in Norway, we were just about to get to our tented camp when the instructor told us we were in a 'white out'.

We were to put our bergens down and follow the instructor. He took us about 600m away to a valley where we were 'stranded' and told to build snow holes! Our entrenching tools were on our bergens as was all our cooking equipment and food. We only had our 'pocket contents' which fortunately in the arctic contain a vast amount of useful stuff. Much like young boys turning out their pockets we got together to work out what we had. We all had to carry a candle in our pockets so we were okay once we managed to dig in; we all had 'emergency rations' in the form of chocolate bars protectively wrapped tightly in tape. I had a spoon so it turned out I would be able to dig a snow hole with it! Gloves, notebook, compass and torch and of course bits of string were also useful items. As we began digging we were informed by the directing staff that our emergency rations were not to be consumed because we might have an emergency! Turns out that deciding when to consume emergency rations is not an individual responsibility and it seemed to me that with rules like this there was a likelihood of finding bodies, starved to death, with emergency rations in their pockets! We manged to dig in and get out of the wind; although there was no 'storm' it was particularly cold when the sun went down. Once inside a snow hole, especially with a couple of people, the shelter provides an element of warmth. The candle burns constantly to ensure there is oxygen getting in and other than making sure you stay awake when on sentry, there is little more to do. The lesson was clear, we had the potential to survive with just our pocket contents and some ingenuity. We also learned that it was important to be able to decide when you were hungry and when it was a real emergency!

Rehearsal

When Chief of Staff in a Regional Division I had to give a presentation to the staff about the closure of the Division. My PA, said that I did not seem nervous when I had given the presentation and answered a series of questions and wondered if I got nervous when speaking to large audiences? I said that I recall reading a book by Dale Carnegie (who also wrote *How to Win Friends and Influence People*) about self-confidence when speaking. My response was a mixture of his advice and my experience, but the bottom line was that preparation was the key. When giving presentations I can be as nervous as the next person, but confidence comes from knowing your subject and preparing well. Think ahead, place yourself in the audience and consider what questions you might ask and prepare the answers. Rehearse the presentation, out loud and with someone listening (or record and play back) if you can so that the first time you 'hear' yourself talking through some of the ideas, is not in front of the audience.

Know your team

An early influence with regard to being prepared was with regard to 'knowing your team'. It was in October 1986 when my Commanding Officer sent a note round to all officers in the Regiment with a copy of a speech made by Field Marshal Sir William Slim to the Sovereign's

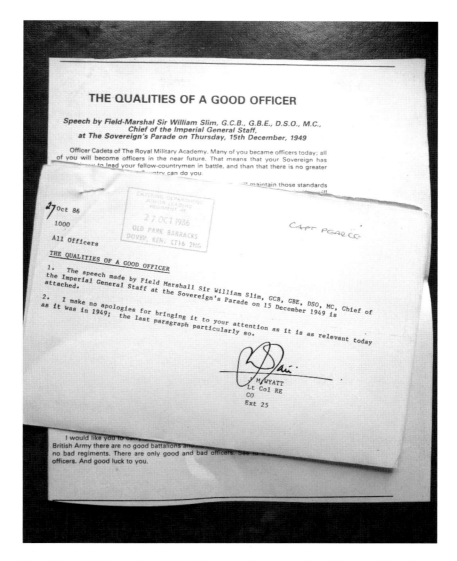

THE QUALITIES OF A GOOD OFFICER

Speech by Field-Marshal Sir William Slim, G.C.B., G.B.E., D.S.O., M.C.,
Chief of the Imperial General Staff,
at The Sovereign's Parade on Thursday, 15th December, 1949

Officer Cadets of The Royal Military Academy. Many of you became officers today; all of you will become officers in the near future. That means that your Sovereign has ...... to lead your fellow-countrymen in battle, and than that there is no greater ....ntry can do you.

.......maintain those standards

27 Oct 86

1000

All Officers

THE QUALITIES OF A GOOD OFFICER

1. The speech made by Field Marshall Sir William Slim, GCB, GBE, DSO, MC, Chief of the Imperial General Staff at the Sovereign's Parade on 15 December 1949 is attached.

2. I make no apologies for bringing it to your attention as it is as relevant today as it was in 1949; the last paragraph particularly so.

M WYATT
Lt Col RE
CO
Ext 25

I would like you to ...... British Army there are no good battalions an...... no bad regiments. There are only good and bad officers. ...... officers. And good luck to you.

Parade on 15 December 1949. The speech was to the officer cadets about to pass out of Sandhurst and be commissioned into the Army and the subject was 'The qualities of a good officer'. Field Marshal Slim had a real affinity and credibility with his soldiers and was highly respected across the ranks. My Commanding Officer circulated the single page to all officers in his Regiment and I have a copy to this day.

I used the speech on an exercise after returning from the war in Iraq and beginning to prepare the Regiment for its redeployment at the end of 2004. I had some new officers in command of the Squadrons and the REME Workshop and the focus of the Command Post Exercise[17] was to review the Standing Operating Procedures (SOPs) and confirm the processes used to plan transport details and vehicle maintenance schedules. I gave a copy of the speech to my sub-unit commanders and asked them to 'explain in a written answer of not more than one side, why you are a good leader'. The particular challenge was that the task was given out at midnight after a long day of planning and the deadline was in two hours. The submitted papers gave me a really good insight into how my new officers were thinking. From one, a typed and detailed analysis of performance against the qualities that Field Marshal Slim had described, to another that repeated and reinforced the qualities without any personal reflection. A third provided a strong and positive assessment of a very self-confident young man and another, neatly hand-written, showed a mature assessment of the strengths and limitations of the individual. A final return with two hand-written sentences suggested that brevity and modesty were the strengths of this officer and that assessment was the role of his superior! There was great value in this exercise for me as it helped to show the character of the leaders in the organisation. Having returned from the Iraq War where I had been privileged to be supported by a very experienced and able crew, a number of my senior officers had departed for their next postings. It was my job now to ensure this next team was prepared for the tasks ahead.

Lesson Nine Summary – Time spent in reconnaissance is seldom wasted

General Bernard Montgomery was known for preparing meticulously, determined not to fight until he thought there had been sufficient preparation for a decisive victory. He would gather resources, prepare detailed plans, train his troops and make personal visits to every unit due to take part in the action.

---

17 Command Post Exercise (CPX), an exercise for those working in the Regimental and Squadron Headquarters; known as 'exercises without troops'.

1. *Do your homework.* We are all busy, but being too busy to prepare properly does a disservice to those who have delivered the work to you. Prioritise your effort; don't get drawn into the G3 all the time.

2. *Read the paperwork.* This lesson is worth repeating; too many do not do it.

3. *Value the organisation above your position.* You are in a privileged position for a temporary period of time. The organisation should run well after you have moved on; ensure your successor starts on the front foot by leaving comprehensive handover notes.

4. *Rehearse.* Confidence comes from knowledge and preparation will ensure success. The military adage, time spent in reconnaissance is seldom wasted certainly rings true for me.

5. *Know your team.* Understand the strengths, weaknesses and character of those in your team.

Supporting Qualities

> **Sometimes we all need the patience of a sniper**
>
> A collection of miscellaneous but important qualities. I have grouped together these thoughts, though each in turn, could be expanded. Essentially, be honest and true yourself and ensure you consider and recognise the efforts of others. Be patient, don't lean in to make decisions or resolve issues your team is wrestling with; help them work the solution and support their development.

Honesty

Honesty is fundamental, not just in leadership but in life. I think that I learned this from my earliest memories. I have found that whether making a decision about a soldier in front of me on 'orders' for a disciplinary episode or talking one-to-one about someone's career, honesty has to be the foundation.

How one conveys an honest message is about consideration, empathy and judgement, but the message has to be honest in the first place. A lesson from well before I can actually remember was told to me by my parents. My father was in the Royal Marines and stationed in Singapore. It was Christmas time and Father Christmas was walking down the street with a big sack of presents calling out the names of children amongst the crowd. When he called mine he said the same as to others 'Now Robert, have you been a good boy this year?' My response followed a period of thinking, and I then replied with 'No, not all the time' as I recalled the many times I had been told off during the year. Father Christmas was somewhat taken aback as all the other children had said yes and been given a present! He saved the day by getting me to promise that I would try harder next year in exchange for the present.

On one posting, I was Chief of Staff of a Regional Division, and essentially posted there to close the Divisional Headquarters. On one of the first gatherings of all the staff I declared that my job was indeed to close the Division. I explained that I was aware there had been rumours about the future of the Headquarters and whether it would close. I said that I would be honest with everyone and tell them what I knew. There was a question about the fact that significant announcements about closures of military units needed to be announced in the House of Commons before they became public and I added a clause to my statement about being honest. I said that if I knew something that was embargoed and I could not tell them the detail, I would tell them that I knew something and it was embargoed! A talk with the Union representative afterwards confirmed that being open and honest with the staff was absolutely the right way to conduct business.

Diplomacy and compromise

When serving in what turned out to be my last Army posting, in the Allied Rapid Reaction Corps (ARRC) I was asked to produce a paper about the NATO Joint Logistic Support Group concept. There were two very different views on the concept from two Brigadier Generals; one from the UK (and my reporting officer) and the other a German Officer responsible for delivering the concept, and the officer I reported to directly day by day. This was a very difficult position but I had been asked by the Lieutenant General commanding the Corps Headquarters to draft a note on the subject that both Brigadiers could sign. I think it was draft eight that eventually went to the Lieutenant General, with two signatures. I considered it a particular success that we managed to get the initially opposing views to a place where both were content.

Compromise and diplomacy are watchwords for me. I believe that we rarely have the opportunity to do what we want. Working through the options and coming to an agreement must be the best way to get buy-in from all involved. This does not mean compromise at all costs, and one should be wary of achieving easy compromise by lowering the bar. The phrase used in NATO when papers are circulated to Nations for comment and agreement is 'silence procedure'. The approach adopted is to circulate the paper, respond to comments or objections from Nations and then re-circulate the document. Agreement is assumed if no comment is received; the 'silence procedure'. This approach can lead to a steady erosion of the initial idea or notion in order to achieve consensus. One should avoid such slippery slopes and aim to achieve success by securing a solution without reducing the ambition.

Value your people

Another thing we did well in the Army, possibly because we did it a lot with most officers rotating on two year tours, was say farewell to people. There was a slightly embarrassing feel to the farewell for one of the longer serving people in the NHS when I saw they were organising their own event. The workplace lunch was a great way for an operational team to take some time out. Having known this person for a couple of years I was privileged to attend. Shortly before the small presentation, I was asked, as the senior person present, to say a few words and present the flowers. After nearly thirty years in the organisation, I was a rather poor substitute but others had put different priorities on their day.

The last person to leave from my organisation in the NATO Headquarters had a pretty good send off, at an accompanied (with partners) event, with senior officers attending and was presented with a picture to remind him of his time in the unit.

Equipment husbandry

There are some routine and downright dull elements of being a leader, inspecting equipment, making sure the routine inspections have been conducted, that it is appropriately stored and maintained. Having said this is dull, it certainly reflects the comment about maintaining standards highlighted by the quote from General Morrison. Equipment management is a leaders' responsibility as much as setting a personal example.

Something drilled into each and every soldier and officer in the Army is the need for good equipment husbandry. Most important of all is looking after your personal weapon; you are taught to clean and look after it over everything else. It is always within arm's reach, you go to great efforts to keep it clean and you sleep with it by your side. Dropping a weapon is a cardinal sin and members of the forces will recollect the punishment press-ups they have done in training after letting their weapon crash to the floor. The weapon is important both because looking after it and handling it properly will mean it is ready to defend you when needed and it also recognises the importance of a piece of equipment designed to kill; a weapon does not know if it is being pointed at the enemy or your buddy. The importance of looking after equipment is tested on exercises and reinforced thorough regular checks and inspections. On the Commando Course I remember one of the tests is a run over an obstacle course of tunnels and mud on Woodbury Common, followed by a march back to the barracks and then a shoot on the range. If your weapon does not fire, if you did not keep it as clean and dry as possible over the obstacles, you will fail the test; getting to the range on time is only part of the challenge, completing the mission on the objective is the key. It becomes second nature to look after your weapon.

Some early lessons stay with me even now and the discipline of 'cleaning the oven' each week was one positive lesson. How many of us just use our ovens but never clean them? As an Apprentice, we stripped them down every Friday, at the end of a week of almost constant work (so maybe that is every couple of months or so in a domestic house I suppose) and cleaned them until they shined like new. It was very much part of the weekly routine, but also instilled in us the need to look after our equipment. I do a lot of triathlon these days and it surprises me how many people turn up for a race with a very dirty looking bicycle. A clean bike is much more likely to be a well maintained one and not let you down in the race with a mechanical failure; the early discipline of keeping your equipment clean and well maintained has served me well, throughout my Army career and during triathlons too.

When deployed with the Allied Command Europe Mobile Force (Land) or AMF(L) as the Officer Commanding the Supply Squadron supporting the UK Element of the Force I was reminded of this attention to detail by my Squadron Quarter Master Sergeant (SQMS). He is the chap responsible for looking after all our stores. We deployed to Norway for three months every winter to conduct a major NATO exercise, testing our people and equipment and demonstrating NATO's collective resolve. Deploying to Norway over winter we clearly needed our Cold Weather equipment but being on NATO stand-by we were, at all times, on short notice to deploy across the NATO region. As a consequence, part of our preparation was to ensure we had all we needed for a deployment to the far eastern border of Turkey with Syria, Iraq and Iran. There are always short-cuts and when packing equipment for Norway, the last thing one might take is green temperate camouflage nets for example. One year, towards the end of our deployment in March, having been in Norway for nearly three months, the Commanding Officer set us the task of driving to the southernmost tip of the country before preparing to fly home. In the planning stage it dawned on us whilst the weather was -20° when north of the Arctic Circle, it was much warmer down south and with a sneaky grin on his face the Commanding Officer reminded us that when we set up our tactical location we were expected to use our green rather than white camouflage! During a three or four day convoy south I was somewhat concerned about being caught out but my SQMS came up trumps and our tented camp location was splendidly decked out in the greenest of green camouflage nets. He clearly understood the Commanders' Intent, but to this day I am not sure how he managed to get so many nets, as I was certain he had not brought them out with us back in December.

I also have a vivid memory of a night convoy in Norway during another one of the winter exercises. We came to a halt on a small road alongside a large lake. The lake was frozen and the recce team went out to drill through the ice and determine the route across. The instruction came back for all vehicles to fit snow chains. The temperature was 'freezing' and I remember walking along the convoy talking to my soldiers as they prepared the vehicles. We had previously been briefed on crossing such obstacles and so opened our doors and windows as we prepared for the crossing. I was in a Landover and therefore felt a little more confident the ice would hold than those in the REME Recovery vehicle ahead of me which weighed over 20 tonnes. Vehicles spaced out and drove slowly down the bank and onto the ice. The noise of our engine did not mask the creaking of the ice and our doors were opened wider. There was not much in the way of conversation in the cab as we looked through the darkness at the small convoy lights on the back of the vehicle ahead reflecting in the water on the surface of the ice. Walking along the convoy on the other side of the lake, the relief was clear as the soldiers removed the snow chains and tried to keep their voices down. The fact that this real test had proved our equipment and preparations clearly gave a boost to the Squadron and demonstrated the value of such training.

Trust in the basics

Another one of the benefits of attending the All Arms Commando Course is that it refines your basic soldier skills. Very late one evening, when my Regiment was on exercise in a German forest, my 2IC and I finished our work in the Command Post (tented headquarters) and crept off into the woods to make our bashers (shelters). It was pitch black. I had a groundsheet, with bungee cords (elastic) attached and lightweight tent pegs fastened to it by cord all stashed in one of the outer pouches of my bergen. Within about two minutes I had this stretched between two trees, pinned at the corners and was underneath and climbing into my sleeping bag. Lying still I heard my 2IC still searching through his bergen trying to find the equipment he needed to sort his Basher. After another ten minutes he whispered, 'Colonel, have you got any spare bungee cords?'

In the NHS there is a significant amount of 'life-saving' equipment which needs to be treated with the right care and attention. It may

not be the mud of Woodbury Common, or the sand and dust in Iraq or Afghanistan, but making sure that equipment is treated with the appropriate care and attention is a fundamental element of making sure we all remain Fit for Role.

Another reminder of the importance of using equipment properly is one of the early briefings we had when on the Commando Course. We were being inspected before an exercise and we had our webbing on; the pouches that contain all you need for the immediate objective rather than your bergen which carried the remainder of your equipment. Each pouch has a use and on the front of the webbing are the ammunition pouches. There are types of exercise that do not need you to carry ammunition; those that test your map reading or speed marches for example. The way this was described has stayed with me and while amusing, the message was very clear.

Ammunition pouches should not contain nutty or sticky (chocolate and sweets) or drinks, they are for ammunition only. The instructor told us that 'ammunition pouches should be full of ammunition, or … empty of ammunition'.

He did not expect to see pouches full or empty of nutty!

The sense that a pouch can be 'empty of' something was not worth the debate but the lesson was clear.

Using equipment for its designated purpose however is another lesson worth reflecting on; how many times have you seen a fire door held open by a fire extinguisher (ironic at least) or some other random doorstop, or reams of paper propping up a computer screen. It's not much of a stretch to use a chair to stand on rather than getting a ladder or set of steps and pressing the earth in a plug socket with a pencil to put a 2 pin plug into a 3 pin socket? I would not wish to stifle innovation, but an important part of 'not walking by' is making sure there is a safe and secure use of equipment. If you notice it, do something about it, don't reflect afterwards that you thought it was not right.

Measurement

One thing that my time at Harvard taught me and the NHS experience has reinforced is the need to make sure you measure the right things when looking at performance or improvement. Take, for example the NHS obsession with the Emergency Department (ED) four hour target. A hospital Trust, with more than 30 different specialist services, over 8000 people and an annual budget of around £500m is deemed effective or not by the performance of its Accident and Emergency Department. On a Quality, Service Improvement and Redesign course I was reminded of the need to ensure the measures identified for a change programme actually showed improvement in the change that was required as we so often default to using metrics that are available. Furthermore, with regard to leadership and management, some work Andrew St George helped with on the subject of Organisational Health[18] in the NHS Trust highlighted the focus we place on the output of an organisation to be the measure of the success of various management processes. If the Emergency Department is hitting its target, the assumption is that all the other aspects of management must be working. I would suggest that leaders need to consider the direction they give and how it is received, communications more generally, accountability, motivation, culture and a host of other elements to measure the 'organisational health' and not just the successful outputs, though of course they are important too.

---

18 Aaron De Smet, Bill Schaninger, Matthew Smith, 'The hidden value of Organisational Health – and how to capture it'. *McKinsey Quarterly*. April 2014.

Fitness

'Mens sana in corpore sano'

A healthy mind in a healthy body is the motto of the Army Physical Training Corps. From the first day I joined as a young Apprentice to the current day I have believed in that notion. Many suggest that when under extreme stress and pressure, the fitter you are the better you will cope. I have been tested at the Royal Military Academy Sandhurst and on the All Arms Commando Course but also on long exercises, challenging operations and many other times in my career. Keeping fit is an individual responsibility and as a leader, being able to make good decisions when cold, wet, tired and hungry is something made somewhat easier if you are physically fit.

7 Transport Regiment had a reputation for being a fit organisation and as Commanding Officer I recall working up a visit programme when the Commander of our Brigade was changing over. Rather than the normal visit to the Squadron lines and a chat with the officers in the Mess, I invited the new Brigadier[19] to attend a Regimental PT

---

19 Brigadier, later Major General D. J. Shouesmith.

session. The Regiment was marching in Squadron groups over a 10 mile circuit, with full equipment, conducting various command tasks on the way. These included First Aid activities and various physical and mental challenges all with a military theme and part of our continued training for the forthcoming deployment to Iraq. The Brigadier arrived, we had a discussion in my office and then both changed for the next phase of the visit. We then ran with a Squadron, the Brigadier able to chat with soldiers and officers on the way, watched them start the Command Task and then caught up with the group just finished and accompanied them to the next task. One comment that stays with me is the PTI (Physical Training Instructor) giving the brief about one of the command tasks. His statement, 'this is a hill, hills are for running up' set me thinking about why hills existed but day-dreaming was short lived as I found myself 'running up' a number of times!

The visit lasted much of the day with a lunch in the field and was a great way of introducing the new Commander to the Regiment.

Mental strength

We should not underestimate the power of the mind when the motivation is strong; I recall talking to my son after he had completed a five-day endurance running event. During the final section, he stopped at a checkpoint in pain. The event doctor's assessment was that he had a stress fracture in his leg. He was advised to pull out. The only way to finish was to walk through the night as he could no longer run due to the injury. One of his proudest moments is captured in the picture of him crossing the finishing line!

Patience

Rushing to the obvious solution is something we all sometimes find ourselves doing, particularly when we are under pressure. There is value in standing back and considering the options; taking time to think through the implications of the solution you may be about to grab. I recall being in the Officers' Mess in Warminster on my Commanding Officers' Designate Course and spending the weekend working in my room. On a sunny Saturday morning my attention was drawn to the window which overlooked the 30 metre range where I saw and heard a sniper cadre being conducted. There was one instructor and four snipers in the prone position on the range; the order was given 'watch and shoot, watch and shoot'. I have been on the ranges many times and normally after that order a target appears within a few seconds and soldiers on the firing point engage and shoot. I watched as the four snipers, camouflaged and lying so still they almost disappeared from my view. I continued to watch and realised that the targets were not going to appear quickly. After a time, I returned to my desk. It must have been well over an hour later when I heard one round fired and went to the window. One target had appeared, one sniper had fired one round. The others were still waiting for their targets to show. Another hour passed and then, suddenly, a single shot. At the window, I saw another target had been revealed, a second sniper had clearly fired, but all four remained absolutely still on the firing point.

We cannot all have the patience of the sniper, but we can all consider the actions we are about to take and think through the consequences before we decide to 'pull the trigger'.

Communications

How many times have you felt left out of the loop when finding out something late in the day. The fundamental lesson from the Army when you receive some information is to ask, 'who else needs to know this?' It is something drilled into all officers when at Sandhurst and I recall being given very clear guidance when being briefed as the duty officer in the Berlin Infantry Brigade Headquarters. While you were the person on duty, there were others 'on call' should you need them. Deciding to call them was your business, but having them find something out in the morning when they ought to have been told during the night when they could do something about it was the risk.

Communications is as much about how it is received as it is about how it is delivered. Empathy and understanding is a critical element and I have certainly fallen foul of this. I pride myself in being diplomatic and seeking successful compromise but have slipped up when adopting 'nudge' tactics. I have found that sending a carefully crafted message, though very clear in my mind, sometimes results in no action or a completely different response than I may have expected.

I have made the assumption that the recipient is thinking about the issue in the way that I was and therefore the gentle nudge should have them responding in an expected manner. When showing an e-mail to a third party recently which in my mind clearly stated my view and I had been upset that the recipient had ignored me; I was told that the e-mail was so subtle that the message was lost. I had not been ignored, simply not conveyed my message clearly. One need not be reminded of the Charge of the Light Brigade in the Crimean war, where confusion about which valley to attack resulted in the 'death of the 600' to know that clear communication is critical to success. There is a balance to be had when communicating; asking everyone if they 'get it' may become tiresome, but sending clear messages is a skill we should all try to refine.

It's not magic!

Many times in the Army and since I have been reminded of the people that keep things going, often unseen, rarely recognised but simply doing their bit for the team. There was a period later in my life where I found myself living on my own. I had a call from my daughter asking if I was surviving and I said I was but the fridge and freezer had broken. Both together, how has that happened she inquired? I explained I had no idea but basically they were both simply empty! Clearly, the magic that had kept them filled over the years had gone!

When I was working in the Army Headquarters in Wilton, I recall a time when it had seriously snowed and people were unable to get to work. The young 'admin assistant' who had the job of ensuring the fridge was stocked with milk lived a couple of bus journeys from the Headquarters and it looked like we would run out that morning.

Just as we were frenetically running around doing our planning, she walked in, having walked all the way from her home because the buses were not running. She put the milk in the fridge and went to her desk, without fanfare.

The story of President John F. Kennedy when he visited the NASA headquarters for the first time in 1961 comes to mind. While touring the facility he introduced himself to a janitor who was mopping the floor and asked him what he did at NASA. The janitor replied, 'I'm helping put a man on the moon!' Having a real understanding of the 'Main Effort' helps to reinforce your part in the whole supply chain.

When we finished an exercise during my tour in the NATO Headquarters in Gloucestershire I recall the German General likened every member of the team to a piece in the workings of an intricate clock. It does not matter if you are the biggest cog in the machine or the smallest spring; every element needs to do the right job to have the clock work and no matter how small, if there is one element missing or not working properly, the clock will not work.

In the Trust Headquarters where I was working, there was a small kitchen where we made the tea and coffee. The milk never ran out! One day when there was no milk first thing, I later mentioned to the person who made sure it was always stocked that the magic had occurred and it was now there if he wanted a drink, fully aware that it was him who had provided it!

Sometimes we take for granted the little things that others put real effort into providing for us; it is not magic, it is people and they deserve a thank you now and again.

Lesson Ten Summary – Sometimes we all need the patience of a sniper

As a logistics officer, I am very aware of the raft of supporting elements to any front line activity. The same applies to leadership, in particular to leaders. Lesson Ten is a grouping of miscellaneous lessons, supporting the fundamentals but without which no organisation can properly function.

> *'You will not find it difficult to prove that battles, campaigns, and even wars have been won or lost primarily because of logistics.'*

> Dwight D Eisenhower

> *'Gentlemen, the officer who doesn't know his communications and supply as well as his tactics is totally useless.'*

> General George S. Patton

1. *Honesty is a fundamental leadership quality.* You build trust from honesty. You cannot be honest sometimes; it must be a thread running through everything you do.
2. *Diplomacy and compromise.* These watchwords help achieve consensus but not through reduced ambition; keep the bar high.
3. *Truly value your people.* Show how much you value your team by devoting your time and effort to them.

4. *Look after your kit.* Management and maintenance of equipment is a critical element of leadership; if you walk by you condone the poor practice.
5. *Fitness.* Keep yourself fit and you will be able to make better decisions when under extreme pressure.
6. *Patience.* Sometimes we all need the patience of a sniper.
7. *Good communication is essential.* Knowledge is power is often quoted, but the opposite is also true, a lack of knowledge leads to a lack of power. Think 'who else needs to know' and convey your message clearly.
8. *When magic happens,* thank those who do it!

Summary: How to Paint a Door

A word on style; not so much a recommendation but more a reflection on my personal style and an observation on those I have seen both in the Army and in the NHS.

I would characterise my style as 'quiet' which many may think is at odds with my military background. I don't believe in shouting, in demanding, in holding to account in a public fashion. I have seen those that do and I acknowledge the success they bring so my approach is not to knock the way others do things. As I have described there are times when the command and control approach is appropriate.

My notion however, is that the 'full-on' approach, the direct challenge, the loud pronouncements and in many cases the creation of a workforce conscious of being monitored all the time can be detrimental to the long term ambitions of many organisations. I prefer to approach things in a collaborative manner, emphasising the power of the team to improve the long term outputs of the organisation; sustaining change rather than delivering immediate but often short-lived improvements.

The trouble with this approach is that it does not meet the demands of impatient regulators, does not appear to be making progress because improvements are incremental and fundamentally take time to deliver. Replacing a failing organisation's Board with an improvement team plays very much to the need to demonstrate action, to ensure visible public accountability and gives a real impression of 'doing something,' but in my mind this does not always deliver sustainable improvements; the new Board will still take time to deliver sustainable change.

Inspiring people to deliver their best, motivating them to work for each other in a collaborative and supportive manner such that they will indeed 'cover your back' and driving change in a quiet and sustainable fashion is the way I have approached my service both in the Army and since leaving.

My daughter responded to a note I sent forwarding a talk by Admiral William McRaven about his book, *First make your bed* by saying her computer had highlighted *The 7 habits of highly effective people* by Stephen Covey. I have read the book before and was reminded of the last habit, about renewal and continual improvement. The notion is there is a need to improve one's personal production capability and in hearing it explained I was reminded about painting a door, more of which later. I claim that there is something more than the achievement of the outputs and that is, improving the process by which they are achieved – giving a better quality output and indeed improving the lot of those engaged in delivering it. Covey states that effectiveness is a function of both production and the capacity to produce and that there is a need for balance between production and production capability and that it applies to the physical, financial and human aspects of an organisation.

Covey uses the fable of the Golden Goose where a poor farmer's goose began laying a golden egg every day, and the farmer soon became rich. He also became greedy and assumed the goose must have many golden eggs within her. In order to obtain all of the eggs immediately, he killed the goose. Upon cutting it open he discovered that it was not full of golden eggs. The lesson is that if one attempts to maximise immediate production with no regard to the production capability, the capability will be lost. I sense that the 'Organisational Health Index'[20] developed by McKinsey is based on this premise; that performance itself is not a measure of a successful organisation and that a measure of the organisation's health is something that can be used to improve the quality of the performance.

---

20 McKinsey & Company, 'The hidden value of organisational health – and how to capture it'. Aaron De Smet, Bill Schaninger and Matthew Smith, *McKinsey Quarterly* April 2014.

In this final chapter I am reminded of an activity I recently undertook having moved house. Not a war story this time, but one that many readers will have encountered in some form or other.

I discovered that the front door needed a bit of attention. I could have painted it within a couple of days and delivered the effect I was after relatively quickly. However, I took the view that I would first inspect the door and its surrounds and soon discovered rot in the skirting board inside the door. I removed the rotten wood and sought to discover where the moisture was getting in and noticed that the seal between the door jamb and the wall was missing in parts and more wood was rotten. This wood removed, I treated the remaining wood with a sealant and then after a few days used wood filler to repair the gaps. A few more days passed and on another dry weekend I sanded down the door, removed the letter-box, taped round the whole thing and applied the undercoat, then the first coat and then the second. Eventually the door was done. It had taken weeks rather than days, but I knew that the root causes of the previous problems were addressed and the new look door would last. It cost more, took longer and now looks the same as a quick application of a coat of paint might have done; you decide which way you wish to do things!

Be true to yourself; do not read management books and try to change into what they recommend but assimilate the advice and guidance into your own style.

The final word must be on motivation. Essentially, we put ourselves through hardship if we are motivated to do so by a cause, a passion or indeed through the inspiration of the leader. I have looked at the essential element of my motivation and believe that throughout my career as a logistician in the Army I have kept in mind the fact that there is a soldier at the end of the supply chain relying on the delivery of the supplies I have provided. Food, fuel, ammunition, spare parts, the aim was to get it to the soldier in the front line. From Factory to Foxhole has been a mantra that has motivated me when cold, wet, tired, hungry or confused. I have tried to convey this commitment to my troops in a range of different appointments and believe that the strength of the message brings out the best in all of us.

In the NHS I found myself using a similar approach. Board to Ward is a comparable ethos that I have used in my short time, suggesting that whatever your role, clinical, managerial or support, you are part of the team that delivers the right care to the patient at the end of the chain.

In schools I encourage every member of the support team to feel, that like the teaching staff, they are contributing to the 'product' which is rounded, grown-up and well-educated young people.

When trying to apply to your own organisation any of the observations or lessons I have captured, the fundamental must be that every member of your staff believes in what you are delivering. Understand the vision of your organisation, what makes it different, what its role or aim is and then convey that sense of purpose to every member of the organisation and you will get the very best from them. They will want to give their very best.

Summary of Lessons

Lesson	Summary
1	Start with the end in view
2	Leadership is a full time job
3	You can't climb a 12-foot wall on your own
4	We all need a sentry to guard us when we sleep
5	Stand still right or wrong
6	Hold your nerve
7	The cost of leadership is self-interest
8	Treat others as you wish to be treated
9	Time spent in reconnaissance is seldom wasted
10	Sometimes we all need the patience of a sniper

1. Start with the end in view

1. *Describe the end state.* This is a challenge with projects and change programmes that often start without a clear understanding of where they are going. In the creative arts world this may well be of value, but in any form of business, describing the objective of the project in clear terms will allow the progress towards it to be measured and more easily corrected if it veers off course.

2. *Don't constrain ideas* at the conceptual stage; but once the mission is written be clear that is exactly what you want to be achieved.

3. *Use Mission Command.* Once the mission is determined, support the initiatives and ideas of your teams; they may find different ways of delivering what you have described. They are closer to the delivery than you are, so give them the freedom to shape their

own route so long as it leads to your destination and meets the timeline.

4. *Resist the temptation to delve into the detail*. It erodes trust and confidence and far from conveying to your troops that you have an understanding of the job they do, it suggests you think you could do it better!

5. *Read the question!* Little more to say, but make sure you are very clear about what you need people to do.

2. Leadership is a full time job

1. *Everything you do will be noticed by your team*. You cannot change what you are but you can be conscious of how you go about your business and how you are perceived by your staff. Walking into head office, sitting at your big desk for the day and walking out will convey a message, but not necessarily the one you wish. Occasionally turning up unexpectedly at the desk or office of members of your team and asking what they are doing will convey a very different message about how you value their contribution.

2. *Set time aside in your diary to talk with members of your team*. Your diary often runs your life and meetings fill the time; book slots for engaging with your team. If they are in the diary they are more likely to happen, but they must be seen as important as other appointments or they will easily be shifted or replaced with other 'more important' events.

3. *Put yourself in the shoes of the person you are about to engage with, interview, talk with....* Listen to their concerns to confirm your assessment, but do the preparation – value them as whole people rather than employees.

4. *If you are in a leadership position, take it seriously*, it is a full time role. It is important to understand the needs of those you lead; put them before your own.

5. *Do your homework* and have the confidence to say your piece and take the lead.

6. *Be prepared to modify your decisions* in light of good evidence.

3. You can't climb a 12-foot wall on your own

1. *Work as a team, you will achieve great things.* Understand the value of the team; remember *you can't climb a 12-foot wall on your own.*

2. *Value the team you have.* The team will operate at the speed of the slowest person, but everyone has skills that may be needed at some point. *Sacrifice your team members at your peril,* you may be losing valuable skills and you may create an atmosphere of scepticism and mistrust.

3. *Treat your team with respect.* Engender a sense of support, encourage people to move from silo working, through good communication and understanding of their part in the overall output.

4. *Every member to contribute.* Hold the team to account; clearly there are times when individuals are rightly responsible and that has its place, but where possible, congratulate teams for their collective action.

5. *Leaders need teams and teams need leaders.* Recognise that you cannot do everything on your own. Ensure every member of the team understands the Main Effort.

4. We all need a sentry to guard us when we sleep

1. *Be true to yourself.* If you have said you will do something, deliver it or tell someone you will not deliver it – before the deadline.

2. *Be confident in your work.* Produce realistic plans and deliver to them; don't provide the answer that is being looked for without the confidence to deliver.

3. *Show confidence in your team.* Trust your people. One person cannot do everything; we all need a sentry to guard us while we sleep. Demonstrate confidence in your team, step off the cliff when they have the rope.

4. *Plan and prepare.* No plan survives contact with the enemy, but it is just irresponsible not to have a plan.

5. Stand still, right or wrong

1. *Identify when or why decisions need to be made; and then make them!* Don't rush to decisions when taking time is appropriate, but don't put them off when a decision is needed.

2. *Follow through with your decisions; make sure they mean something to your team.* Hold people to account, when decisions are made, they should be supported by the whole team.

3. *Plan ahead; know when decisions are needed and support your team by making them.* Think through what advice you would give to others if facing the same challenge. Don't get backed into a corner. Consider Question Four.

4. *Spend time working out when a decision needs to be made.* Delaying a decision for a specific reason is acceptable, putting off decisions is not.

6. Hold your nerve

1. *Choose your moments*; don't confuse stubbornness with resilience.

2. Leadership is more than being in charge, it's about *having the mental and physical strength* to make decisions and stand by them.

3. *Be determined in seeing things through to a conclusion.* If you are made responsible for something then take control of how you will deliver it.

4. *Maintain a sense of humour.* Of the four elements of the Commando Spirit – Courage, Determination, Unselfishness and Cheerfulness in the face of adversity – the last is what gets people through the darkest moments. Maintain a sense of perspective.

5. *Know your team.* Recognise the challenges they face and the impact they may have on them; consider the whole person not just the element you see at work. Know them sufficiently well to notice behavioural changes.

7. The cost of leadership is self-interest

1. *Accept authority and take responsibility from day one.* Do not pass blame for the shortcomings of your team. Jim Collins believes great leaders blend 'extreme personal humility with intense professional will'.

2. *Decisions made by your predecessor are now yours to own.* If you do not agree, change things, but don't hide behind decisions made by others.

3. *Use the evidence available.* If you have reference data, information or evidence, read it thoroughly before taking a decision.

4. *Speak up if you think something is wrong.* But don't just criticise, offer a solution. If you are going to question a decision, think through the options.

5. *Decide where you will have the best effect.* Being responsible does not necessarily mean go to the point of action; indeed taking the wider view may give you a better understanding of the overall situation.

8. Treat others as you would wish to be treated

1. *Trust your team; they will trust you.* Demonstrate trust in your team; treat people as you would wish to be treated.
2. Don't underestimate the *power of empowerment.*
3. *Value challenge.* Listen and react to challenge from a member of your team in the way you would wish your boss to value your challenge.
4. *Apply the 'one third/two thirds' rule to planning.*
5. *Speak up,* but don't criticise without contributing to the delivery of a solution.

9. Time spent in reconnaissance is seldom wasted

1. *Do your homework.* We are all busy, but being too busy to prepare properly does a disservice to those who have delivered the work to you. Prioritise your effort; don't get drawn into the G3 all the time.
2. *Read the paperwork.* This lesson is worth repeating; too many do not do it.
3. *Value the organisation above your position.* You are in a privileged position for a temporary period of time. The organisation should run well after you have moved on; ensure your successor starts on the front foot by leaving comprehensive handover notes.
4. *Rehearse.* Confidence comes from knowledge and preparation will ensure success. The military adage, time spent in reconnaissance is seldom wasted certainly rings true for me.
5. *Know your team.* Understand the strengths, weaknesses and character of those in your team.

10. Sometimes we all need the patience of a sniper

1. *Honesty is a fundamental leadership quality.* You build trust from honesty. You cannot be honest sometimes; it must be a thread running through everything you do.

2. *Diplomacy and compromise.* These watchwords help achieve consensus but not through reduced ambition; keep the bar high.

3. *Truly value your people.* Show how much you value your team by devoting your time and effort to them.

4. *Look after your kit.* Management and maintenance of equipment is a critical element of leadership; if you walk by you condone the poor practice.

5. *Fitness.* Keep yourself fit and you will be able to make better decisions when under extreme pressure.

6. *Patience.* Sometimes we all need the patience of a sniper.

7. *Good communication is essential.* Knowledge is power is often quoted, but the opposite is also true, a lack of knowledge leads to a lack of power. Think 'who else needs to know' and convey your message clearly.

8. *When magic happens,* thank those who do it!

Commanding Officer's Letter of Intent – 11 July 2003

On taking over command I wanted to start by making clear my values and standards. In particular with regard to my approach to Mission Command and in order to encourage empowerment and initiative, ensure that my direction was clear, and thus enable and inspire decision making without constant reference the Commanding Officer. What follows is a copy of the letter I sent to every officer in the Regiment and to the Regimental Sergeant Major as I took command.

1. Introduction. Firstly, I wish to register my appreciation for the excellent handover programme and indeed for the very high standard of administration evident in the unit. I have certainly taken over an organisation in good order and wish to assure you all that my intent for my first few months in post is to get to know the people in the Regiment and gain a better understanding of the processes and procedures currently in being. We evidently do not need to conduct any major repair work, but like any vehicle, continued maintenance is the only way to ensure reliable performance.

2. Having now completed my second week in Command I felt it appropriate to write a note giving my views on a number of key issues that affect the soldiers and officers in the Regiment.

3. Ethos. To encapsulate the ethos of the Regiment in a single phrase I offer the following:

A highly professional unit ready for operations
in which soldiers and families enjoy serving.

But this may be over simplified and I add the following notes:

    a. Professional. This implies the pursuit of the highest standards of professional excellence and the delivery of high quality output. It does not imply that we should seek perfect solutions, nor that mistakes are unacceptable (people who do not make mistakes are either not trying hard enough or not learning). But it does mean that I require you to ensure that we are individually mentally and physically robust and fit for role; that we are appropriately manned, trained and prepared for task, that we are individually and collectively confident in our ability and that we bring to bear every ounce of personal and team effort to produce the best possible outputs on time.

b. Readiness. We are to be at the appropriate readiness state as directed by Commander 102 Log Brigade. This requires equipment to be maintained to a high standard and an ability to operate 24 hours a day for extended periods of deployment whilst remaining fresh and effective.

4. Intent. In order to convey my personal views on a number of subjects I have listed some below. This does not necessarily mean that this is the only way to do something, but it does give a start point for any discussions we may have in the future:

a. Team. Team is a key word. We must function as a team to deliver against those tasks set for us by Brigade. I require total commitment from individuals to their team and a selfless consideration for others. I also require you to look after our team and consider their safety as a very high priority, to treat them fairly, to ensure they take their leave entitlement and that they have proper opportunities for personal and physical training.

b. Leadership. Leaders lead (from the front, by personal example). You do not need to be the fittest, the fastest or the most technically able – but you must take part, demonstrate commitment and show determination. Officers should recall the qualities of commanders taught at Sandhurst: Leadership, Professional Knowledge, Vision and intellect, Judgement and initiative, Courage and resolve, Self Confidence, the ability to Communicate, Integrity and Example.

Included in Leadership is the requirement to make decisions. These must be made having taken advice and following the appropriate research or investigation. Issues may, indeed in most cases should, be discussed, but once a decision has been made then it should be supported and implemented, by all, without further question. There is no room for continued criticism, 'I don't agree either but we have to do it this way' only breeds discontent and undermines the cohesion of the team. Have your say at the appropriate time and then implement the eventual decision with wholehearted support and by doing so you will find your decisions supported equally – from those above and below you.

c. Responsibility. An extract from ADP Volume 2 Command: Responsibility is a unique concept. It can only reside and inhere in a single individual. You may share it with others, but your portion is not diminished. You may delegate it, but it is still with you. You may disclaim it, but you cannot divest yourself of it.

I believe that those who have responsibility should take it seriously – I do. If things go wrong then those responsible should be able to stand up with confidence and explain how they set the procedures in place to prevent the accident or incident. Only then will we learn and improve our procedures in the future. Whilst I take overall responsibility for all that happens in this Regiment, I am not able to do everything myself and therefore rely on those given specific appointments to do their jobs in a responsible and effective manner. If you are not sure of the task you are responsible for, then ask for further guidance – if you are sure, then do it to the best of your ability.

d. Communication. The only way we manage to conduct any form of business is through accurate and timely communication. You are responsible for making sure that messages are passed in the appropriate manner and for representing views through the chain of command. How often do we hear that a soldier was 'not aware', 'not briefed' or simply just was not told? We must all put considerable effort into making good communication a priority. Messages must be clear, seek guidance if they are not, and pass them through the chain of command with your complete support.

e. Discipline. There is a robust but fair system in place and I wish that it should continue. I have examined the existing policies and visited the Guard Room and am confident that we have the necessary processes in place to treat soldiers in accordance with the current regulations. We must continue to take this issue seriously and enforce the robust system, within the new rules, and with action being taken at the appropriate level (not all cases need to be referred to the CO). We must also operate within the strict rules and regulations and under the watchful 'eagle' eye of OSCA[21] and I know that the Adjutant and RSM are planning to conduct a Discipline Study Day in the near future. This requires cases to be thoroughly investigated at the lowest level with a scrupulous attention to detail.

f. Family. We all have families. This is not just the married accompanied soldier, single soldiers have parents,

---

21 Army Legal Services regulatory body.

brothers, sisters and relationships with girlfriends/ boyfriends. The contribution families make to the well-being of the Regiment is significant and should be properly recognised. The Army policy is to encourage accompanied service. We must play our part in providing this encouragement. Soldiers and families should enjoy serving in 7 Regiment and feel that their contribution is appreciated and recognised. This means a friendly atmosphere in the families' office, family events for the Regiment and in the messes, good communication between the Regiment and the families, indeed a general ethos of 'inclusion'.

g. Service. Consider your soldiers before yourself.

h. Discrimination and Diversity. Discrimination – including positive discrimination, will not be tolerated. All people should be treated fairly and equally. The publication on 'Values and Standards of the British Army' is quite clear, please read it.

i. Safety. The responsibility or the safety of our soldiers does not lie solely with the Unit Health and Safety Officer. The safety of all personnel in the Regiment should be a high priority, particularly for those organising events or activities. Ask questions, check qualifications, consider the 'what if' scenario. We may well be in a 'risk' business but the death of a soldier through the negligence of his superiors is unacceptable.

j. Fitness. I put a high priority on fitness. The BPFA[22] is the minimum standard and individuals should be able to

---

22 Basic Physical Fitness Assessment.

reach the required standard, at all times, without pre-training. This will be tested. See 'Leadership' above.

    k. Efficiency. An efficient and effective unit provides the best for the soldiers, their professional development, their families and their welfare. Efficiency can be as simple as meeting deadlines, sending holding replies whilst work is in hand and making sure telephones are answered or diverted rather than ringing and being ignored.

5. Summary. I have not produced this note to impose my personality on every aspect of the running of the Regiment, but issue it to ensure that, with a 'Mission Command' approach you are all aware of the 'Commanders Intent'. I wish to encourage participation, innovation and initiative at all levels. I am prepared to discuss new ideas, or indeed challenges to my current thinking – and also believe that following discussion (if necessary and appropriate) once a decision is made we all support it in a professional manner as if the decision was our own.

Director of Operations, Medicine Division, Gloucestershire Hospitals Foundation Trust. Approach – April 2016

How do I work: essentially with an open door – both in a physical sense and through a willingness to consider different ways of doing things. Good ideas often falter due to process and I will be determined in my efforts to help you bring the changes needed to make our outputs better for the patients we serve.

Leadership. Demonstrate how you wish things to be by your actions:

'the standards you walk past are the standards you accept'[23]

Communications. It is important that we all have the right information at the right time and we all have the same message; I will endeavour to ensure the communication lines are effective and timely.

Teamwork. We clearly need to work as a team, supporting each other in order to ensure we avoid duplication in process and deliver an efficient and coherent output:

'none of us is as strong as all of us'[24]

Responsibility. We all have to take responsibility, make decisions; seek authority where you feel you do not currently hold it and raise to the next level where appropriate.

Reliability. Attend meetings on time. Deliver the output on time. If you cannot make a deadline, tell someone, before the deadline!

Productivity. Productivity is a critical determinant of cost efficiency. We are constantly asked to seek greater efficiency and I believe that one element we must review is the variation in productivity. Where we see best practice, we should try and emulate it.

Decisions. Decisions sometimes need to be made in a timely fashion which means that all the desired information and evidence may not be available. If a decision is time critical, then a decision should be made,

---

23 Lt Gen David Morrison, Chief of the Australian Army, 2013.

24 *Winning* by Sir Clive Woodward, 2004.

based on the evidence available at that time and the best judgement of those making the decision.

Planning. None of us like surprises; think ahead, plan and make contingency plans for when the plan, inevitably, does not work!

Celebration. We must recognise where people have put in that extra effort, value those delivering under difficult circumstances and celebrate when we do good things. I am an optimist and will seek to maintain the 'glass half full' perspective; not spin, but recognition of the hard efforts that deliver our outputs each and every day.

Letters from the Commanding Officer on Operation TELIC (Iraqi Freedom) 2003

7 Transport Regiment was a Third Line organisation providing transport and fuel support to the Division, delivered through Second Line logistic units. The Regiment was part of 102 Logistic Brigade and provided 60 Heavy Equipment Transporters (HET) to transport Armour, Artillery and Engineer equipment, Fuel support in 55 Tanker vehicles and a capacity of some 5 million litres in static tanks, and General Transport with 150 DROPS[25] vehicles. The Regiment deployed in early 2003 as the sole Third Line logistic Regiment, taking under command 3 additional task squadrons[26], with a total manpower count of some 1200 soldiers

These four letters were sent from Lieutenant Colonel G. R. Pearce MBE, Commanding Officer, 7 Transport Regiment Royal Logistic Corps. Addressed to the Second in Command, all Squadron Commanders, the Officer Commanding the Regimental Workshop, the Adjutant and Operations Officer. Written from the Regimental Headquarters in the desert location, at Centurion Lines, Umm al 'Aysh, Kuwait, British Forces Post Office 662.

---

25 Dismountable Rack Offload and Pickup Dystem. The total capacity was 150 'trains' (a DROPS vehicle and trailer).

26 A DROPS Squadron (28 QOGLR), An Engineer and Water Squadron and a General Transport Squadron from the RAF (2 MT Squadron [70 vehicles]).

Letter One – Dated 19 February 2003

'You are the people to make it happen'[27]

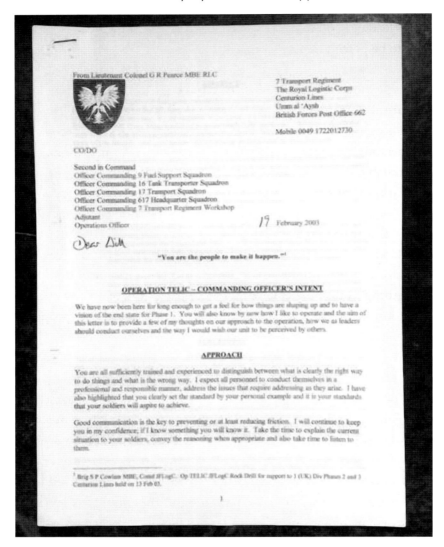

OPERATION TELIC – COMMANDING OFFICER'S INTENT

We have now been here for long enough to get a feel for how things are

—

27 Brigadier S P Cowlam MBE, Comd JFLogC. Op TELIC JFLogC Rock Drill for support to 1 (UK) Div Phases 2 and 3. Centurion Lines held on 13 Feb 03.

shaping up and to have a vision of the end state for Phase 1. You will also know by now how I like to operate and the aim of this letter is to provide a few of my thoughts on our approach to the operation, how we as leaders should conduct ourselves and the way I would wish our unit to be perceived by others.

APPROACH

You are all sufficiently trained and experienced to distinguish between what is clearly the right way to do things and what is the wrong way. I expect all personnel to conduct themselves in a professional and responsible manner, address the issues that require addressing as they arise. I have also highlighted that you clearly set the standard by your personal example and it is your standards that your soldiers will aspire to achieve.

Good communications is the key to preventing or at least reducing friction. I will continue to keep you in my confidence; if I know something you will know it. Take the time to explain the current situation to your soldiers, convey the reasoning when appropriate and also take time to listen to them.

CONDUCT

This operation will give you both great opportunity to command and gain experience in a war fighting scenario and will at the same time be testing to each of you. Your main task is to lead your soldiers as well as you can. We are currently in the throes of a very testing deployment with the RSOM[28] of the UK Force being conducted in an extremely tight timeframe. We have a significant task; to ensure that the deployment and sustainment of the UK Force meets the Coalition timeline – there will be friction – and good leaders will resolve the problems and produce solutions.

---

28 Reception, Staging and Onward Movement. A military term used to describe the early elements of a deployment process, setting the conditions for any subsequent operations.

- You must lead by example, the way you conduct yourself is as important as the way you command. I put great store on leading by example and believe that your personal stance will be adopted by your soldiers; if you cut corners, your soldiers will.

- Be calm. When a problem comes to you it is because it has not been resolved at the lower level. Keep a level head, explore the options and make a clear decision for your soldiers to follow.

- Loyal. The friction will increase and we can all be tempted to 'blame others'. I am not suggesting you try to convince your soldiers that all is well, but our task is to work as a team and achieve the required end state – 1 (UK) Division crossing the Line of Departure in good order and on time. Support the Chain of Command, raise issues where and when appropriate but also support the decisions that are made by our higher command.

- Take Responsibility. You are in Command. You are responsible for your soldiers; for their safety, for their lives. Take the responsibility seriously, consider the impact of the orders you give and ensure that you have considered all options and consequences before you give them. Know your soldiers, look after their health and welfare – put them **first**.

- Be honest.

PERCEPTION

The attitude you portray has a direct effect on all personnel around you. Be aware of the perception others have of you because if you are positive, they will be. It does not mean you should say you can do things when they are not possible but those jobs which are more difficult or unpleasant (but still have to be done) will get done more quickly and will have less of a negative effect on those doing them.

We are all living in the same place; we share the same accommodation, food, ablutions and have the same safety and health requirements, most importantly the jobs we have to achieve are for the Regiment as a whole, and therefore the responsibility of all of us. Help those who seek it and if you have the spare capacity, offer help to those who are working when you are not. You may find the favour is returned when you need it.

Make everyone welcome. Every person who visits is a potential source of help or advice; making them welcome and taking time to brief them and help them will make them more likely to return the favour in the future. By not doing so the opposite is true.

The impression we create is a combination of the professional approach from every individual in the Regiment. The reputation we have is good, we need to maintain it, indeed we should strive to improve it where possible. Though it is gained by the hard efforts of every individual, it can be lost by the poor performance of only one. I rarely receive reports of the number of excellent convoy drills that I have seen, but do get informed of the 7 Regiment soldier, speeding down the Sixth Ring smoking a cigarette. It is important that we operate as a team, that every member of the Regiment contributes to the team effort and that we are all aware of the impact our good, and bad, performance will have on the corporate image of the Regiment.

The old adage 'You never get a second chance to make a first impression' is true. The impression a person has when they arrive in a location, meet you or your soldiers for the first time or receive a brief from you will be an impression that remains with them for some time. The right impression will ensure that any visitors leave with a sense that 7 Transport Regiment is a professional Regiment with a positive 'can do' attitude who will take the time to help others and make them welcome.

SUMMARY

The responsibility you have on this operation as leaders and commanders is significant. You are also privileged to be in command at this time. If you are uncertain, ask. Whilst I am keen for commanders to have the freedom to operate and work within the framework of Mission Command, I also conduct an 'open door' approach and am happy, indeed I prefer to discuss issues before decisions are made. I have stated that you have responsibility but this does not transfer to you the ultimate responsibility for the Regiment. You each have a significant part to play in the success of our contribution to this operation, you each have my confidence and support.

Letter Two – Dated 22 March 2003

OPERATION TELIC – RISK
'Manage, assess and take risk'[29]

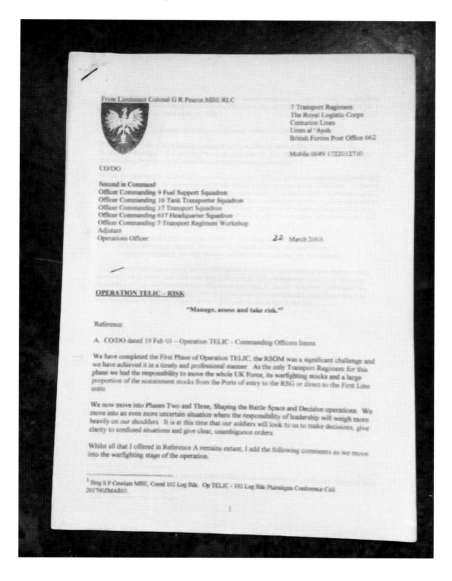

---

29 Brig SP Cowlam MBE, Comd 102 Log Bde. Op TELIC – 102 Log Bde Ptarmigan Conference Call 201700ZMAR03.

We have completed the First Phase of Operation TELIC, the RSOM was a significant challenge and we have achieved it in a timely and professional manner. As the only Transport Regiment for this phase we had the responsibility to move the whole UK Force, its warfighting stocks and a large proportion of the sustainment stocks from the Ports of Entry to the RSG[30] or direct to the First Line units.

We now move into Phases Two and Three, Shaping the Battle Space and Decisive operations. We move into an even more uncertain situation where the responsibility of leadership will weigh more heavily on our shoulders. It is at this time that our soldiers will look to us to make decisions, give clarity to confused situations and give clear, unambiguous orders.

Whilst all that I offered in Reference A[31] remains extant, I add the following comments as we move into the warfighting stage of the operation.

I have mentioned on a number of occasions that I 'predict confusion'. I have said that it is the task of the leader to expect uncertainty, resolve difficulties and give clear guidance and orders to his soldiers. ADP[32] 2 – Command, states that:

A commander should accept the inevitability of confusion and disorder.

Friction, that 'force that makes the apparently easy so difficult', adds further to the chaos and confusion of conflict[33]. It is your task to see through this fog, in a calm manner identify and assess the situation, formulate your plan and convey your orders with clarity.

Before we deployed from Bielefeld I asked each of you to bring a 'pocket of military judgement and one of flexibility'. We have

---

30 Rear Support Group. A desert location where the Third Line Stocks were held for the UK Division.

31 The first letter dated 19 February 2003.

32 Army Doctrine Publication.

33 Carl von Clausewitz, *On War*, edited and translated by Michael Howard and Peter Paret. Princeton University Press, 1976, p. 121.

reached deeply into the flexibility reserves during Phase One. Whilst we need to maintain the supply we now also need to apply military judgement, based on the information you have available at the time, your understanding of the commander's intent and your own previous experience. Drivers will be tired. Vehicles, whilst being maintained to a high standard will start to be used when in a 'battleworthy'[34] condition, we will receive short notice tasks and planned ones will take longer to complete than expected.

The willingness to take calculated risks, is an inherent aspect of resolve but requires military judgement. Although the inherent element of chance in war cannot be eliminated, the risks may be reduced by foresight and careful planning[35].

As leaders you must accept that you may not always have all the information you require to make decisions; this is where your understanding of the 'intent' is important and where thorough knowledge of your soldiers, their strengths and weaknesses, is crucial. You have guidelines, you have experience from exercises and other operations and you now have the task of providing the very best transport and fuel support to the soldiers on the front line in this war.

---

34 A formal declaration that the vehicle is below a peacetime standard but safe to use in a warfighting environment.

35 ADP 2 Command – Apr 95. Chapter 2.

Letter Three – Dated 12 April 2003

OPERATION TELIC – THE MIDDLE GAME

The effectiveness of any CSS[36] system is dependent upon accurate and timely reporting, clearly defined procedures, adequate communications, good liaison and a clear understanding of the operational plan.[37]

We are now well into the middle of the operation; Phase One, the RSOM was a period of extensive activity and Phase 2 and 3 have required significant sustainment support. We now find ourselves providing 'more of the same' and it is at this time that leadership qualities will be tested. Soldiers are 'Theatre Experienced', they know the routes in Kuwait and Iraq and the units they deal with and more recently the NBC threat from conventional forces is much reduced. As soldiers relax, some transport details and duties become routine, the chances of a reduction in our standards, or worse, of accidents will increase.

The operation itself and our tour in particular are far from over. We deployed on a declared six month tour and we must maintain the high standards we have set from the beginning throughout the deployment. We expect much of our soldiers:

The country expects soldiers to be available at any time, to go anywhere and to carry out a wide variety of potential missions in support of government policy, often as the last resort. Such capability requires good equipment, organisation, training and leadership, and above all, soldiers with high degrees of personal and collective commitment, self-sacrifice, forbearance and mutual trust. Together these cement the morale and teamwork so essential for operational success. This demands hard and realistic

---

36 Combat Service Support. Abbreviation used for logistics.

37 British Military Doctrine – Application of Force. Army Code 71622 dated 1998. Chapter 6, Section 8, paragraph 104.

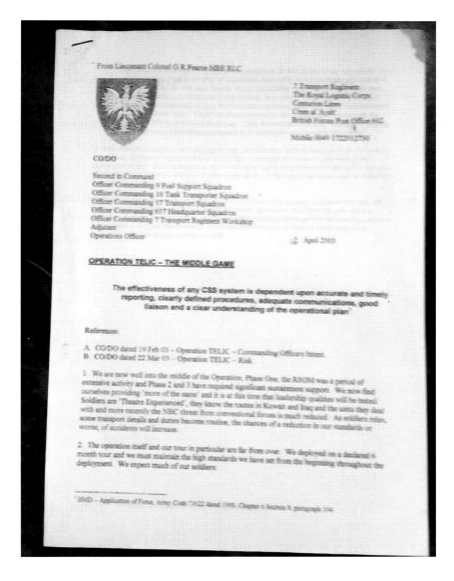

training, the unquestioning acceptance of authority and sound discipline[38].

Whilst the requirement to provide support may become more stable there is no scope for leaders, at any level, to relax or reduce their grip

38   ADP Vol 5 – *Soldiering, The Military Covenant* – Chapter 1, Para 0102.

on the daily operations we conduct. The lives of our soldiers are no less valued in this phase than in any other and it is our business to ensure we maintain all the checks and balances required to ensure their safety. I will not repeat the message in Reference A, but I do urge all of you to read it again.

Finally, as the deployment continues people will become tired, as tasks are repeated people will be less tolerant of mistakes or delays. Again, the leader must stand back from the heat and see through to the issue – we are here to support the deployed Brigades and whilst the Iraqi Regime may have collapsed, they are still in contact, the asymmetric threat is real and we must continue to provide the very best logistic support possible.

Letter Four – Dated 22 May 2003

OPERATION TELIC – THE CONCLUSION

The roulement phase is far more complex than anything we have done so far with more moving pieces and forces moving in and out of Theatre at the same time[39]

I have issued the plan for our Post Operational Tour Leave with the intent for the majority of people to be on leave during the block period and to minimise the numbers away during the training periods. I have also issued the Interim Training Directive for the second half of the year, in advance of the Brigade Operations and Training Plan, expected in the near future. Whilst we eagerly and rightly look forward to a period of well-earned leave we must also start to plan for the hard training that is required in the second half of this year. The first element of the training is the rehabilitation of our vehicle fleet. As a transport Regiment we must ensure that the tools of our trade are maintained to the very highest standards. I know much has been done already out here on the operation, both in the Squadrons and in the Workshop, we have identified the spares required for the rehabilitation period in September and should now plan the detail of the work programmes for the period.

Whilst our attention turns to redeployment, we should not underestimate the size of the task that remains, we still have the majority of our drivers on detail and the roulement of the Division and its Brigades will continue to keep us busy, particularly as we handover to 27 Regiment at the same time. Safety is the business of commanders at all levels; safety when your soldiers are at work, rest and play. I emphasise the requirement to oversee safety briefings, to ensure soldiers wear seatbelts at all times but it is also important that safety is uppermost in our minds when at rest in the camp locations as well as when soldiers are relaxing or playing sport. The temperatures continue to rise and although we are acclimatised we

---

39   Brig I Dale MSc Bsc (Eng) CEng MIEE, Comd JFLogC during the Backbrief following the staff estimate on the Roulement of Headquarters 1 and 3 Division, 7 and 19 Brigade an up to 7000 personnel from Multinational contributions.

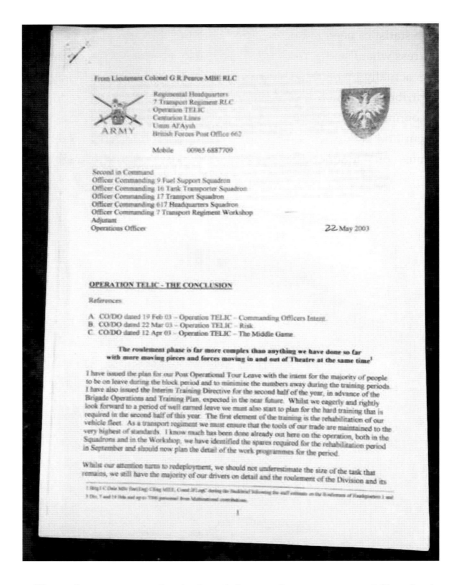

still need to manage physical training and ensure our soldiers look out for each other. We also have a responsibility during the handover to 27 Regiment to ensure their soldiers are properly advised on how to avoid heat illness, based on the advice issued in formal publications and our own recent experiences.

The Regiment has achieved a great deal in this deployment, the only Third Line Regiment for Phase 1 and now again for Phase 4.

The statistics need not be repeated here but they are impressive and I stress what I said at the Parade last week; it is not the Regiment that has actually made these achievements, it is each individual soldier's contribution – and that contribution has been significant. They deserve recognition for a job well done whilst we must continue to look after them and ensure we finish our part in this operation in the same professional manner that we have conducted ourselves throughout.

Endorsements

Brigadier Al Deas MBE (Commandant of the Defence College of Logistics and Personnel Administration, Director Skills for Logistics)
It is entertaining and highly relevant to any leadership institution.
….it was a great read and this will be a publication worthy of the attention of leadership organisations around the world.

PS. I now know why I was never getting my stuff on time in Iraq – you were sitting back with the showers drinking tea and eating custard creams with your adjutant!

Steve Bonser (Head of Operations, Aneurin Bevan University Health Board and former Lance Corporal, Royal Corps of Signals)
A fascinating and well written book clearly highlighting how contrasting the UK Military and NHS leadership styles are. It articulates through experiences and descriptive anecdotes how they can be easily transposed for everyday use at every level of management.

A book that every aspiring leader should read and refer to throughout their career.

Lieutenant Colonel (Retired) Tracy (Peejay) Price-Jones (Chief Instructor and Head of Equality and Diversity at the Centre of Defence Leadership and Management)
We cannot all be elite soldiers or Generals and while reading about their journeys may inspire us, achieving such greatness remains in the realms of fantasy for all but the few. This book is about

practical leadership lessons that apply to the many – we can apply these lessons whatever sector we work in to get the best from our teams.

Learned at the 'university of life' this is a valuable collection of lessons for young people aspiring to any kind of leadership role.

Major General Julian Free CBE (Chief of Staff Allied Rapid Reaction Corps; Commandant Joint Services Command and Staff College, The Defence Academy of the United Kingdom; Deputy Vice Chancellor University of Lincoln)

An enjoyable book of short stories and anecdotes, which illustrate a lifetime's learning. Young people in many sectors will gain from the insights and lessons and can draw on this experience as they enter the world of work and leadership roles in particular.

Dr Joanna Bayley (CEO Gloucester GP Consortium Ltd. Clinical Lead and Business Manager GDoc Ltd)

This is a book that deserves a wide readership. Its lessons on how to be an effective leader – engagingly presented – are valuable to many professions and to every stage of a career.

Dr Shera Chok (GP and Associate Medical Director, Derbyshire Community Health Services NHS Foundation Trust)

Bob – your book is fabulous and gives an insight into the life of the young Colonel. We need more of the values you talk about in these difficult times.

Stephen Hart (National Director of Leadership Development NHS Leadership Academy)

In my experience, and to my knowledge, healthcare and military leaders are the best our society has to offer. They face intransigent and complex problems and they do so in an environment of constrained resources, political imperative, public scrutiny and moral duty. I am in awe of all of them. This pocket guide draws on Bob's personal experience and knowledge in both sectors, it will be a useful reference guide for leaders at every level of health and care and beyond.'

Jack M. Williams eighteen years old. ARTSED. BA Hons Student.
I found the book an easy and enjoyable read written in a clear way for me to understand. Mixing real life experiences with theories, views, values and ideas.

Teamwork and Leadership. Sometimes challenges seem so big but this book outlines that the right attitude, preparation and respect are vital to achieving one's goals. It reminded me and reinforced my views of the importance of respectful teamwork which in my studies is so important.

I will most certainly use some of the messages in this book through my studies at university.

For more information and details

of speaking opportunities contact:

bob@12ftwall.com